All about Children's Church

All about Children's Church
by
Barbara Wilkerson

Christian Publications, Inc.
Harrisburg, Pennsylvania

Christian Publications, Inc.
25 S. 10th Street, P.O. Box 3404
Harrisburg, PA 17105

The mark of 𝒞𝒫 *vibrant faith*

Library of Congress Catalog Card Number: 80-70732
© 1981 by Christian Publications, Inc. All rights reserved
ISBN: 0-87509-295-0
Scripture quotations from the New American Standard Bible, ©
The Lockman Foundation 1960, 1962, 1963, 1968, 1971, 1972, 1973,
1975, are used by permission.
Quotations from THE NEW INTERNATIONAL VERSION, NEW
TESTAMENT © 1973 by the New York Bible Society International are used by permission.
Quotations from the *Berkeley Version*, Zondervan Publishing House, © 1959, used by permission.
Quotations from the *Jerusalem Bible* are used by permission of Doubleday and Company.
Quotations marked LB are taken from *The Living Bible*, paraphrased, (Wheaton: Tyndale House, 1971) and are used by permission.
Printed in the United States of America

Contents

Introduction 6

1. How a Child Worships: Acceptably 7
2. How a Child Learns: According to His Way 27
3. Questions You May Have about Children's Church 53
4. Providing an Environment for Worship 73
5. Preparing for Worship 90
6. Activities for Learning and Worship 107
7. Time for Worship 129
8. The Elements of Worship 140

   Appendix 168

Introduction

The church that seeks to completely serve its congregation must have a ministry to children, for the childhood years are important for teaching and evangelizing. Too many churches are satisfied with a baby-sitting service rather than with having a well-planned and well-executed children's ministry. This lack of purpose can only be corrected when the leadership understands the biblical basis for reaching children.

The Sunday school is a teaching agency for children. Some churches also have clubs organized to integrate Bible knowledge with other activities of interest to children. The equivalent of the adult worship, however, is not always provided. Children's church is the answer to that need. Children's church is essentially children at worship.

The success of such a service depends on having knowledgeable and well-trained workers to conduct it. They must understand the special worship needs of children and how these differ from those of adults. The resources, facilities, and other outward equipment may be the best, but the program cannot be effective unless the leadership can adapt biblical principles to the age level of those attending children's church.

A good children's church results from training, planning, and praying while keeping the scriptural purpose in full view. Workers will be effective if they learn the age characteristics of the children with whom they will be working, formulate clear objectives for the ministry, and prepare and plan each service with the objectives in mind. Reaching these teaching goals requires commitment, discipline, and diligent study. Adult leaders will find such a devoted ministry to children to be rewarding and challenging.

1

How a Child Worships: Acceptably

Eight-year-old Andrew bounced into Children's Church, as delighted to be back as we were to see him. "Andrew," the leader exclaimed, "we've missed you! Come have a seat."

Andrew joined our circle and entered into the worship service with characteristic enthusiasm. Later he told me, in perceptive language, the reason for his long absence: "We were going to another church for a while. You know that one on our corner? But there I had to go to grown-up church. My mom said it seemed like in that church, children were just an afterthought."

Ask five pastors or lay workers why they have a children's church program, and you will come up with five different answers.

"We needed to relieve overcrowding in the pews."

"It frees parents to concentrate on worship, sing in the choir, usher, and so forth."

"All the churches in this area seem to be doing it."

"We have a lot of bus children whose parents don't come to church."

"Sunday school just doesn't seem to provide enough teaching time."

Few leaders mention the best reason—in fact, the only valid reason—for providing a separate service for children: it helps them worship. If this were not so, it would be hard to justify removing children from the rest of the congregation. It is good for children to sit with their families. It is good for them to experience the fellowship of the body of Christ in the sanctuary. But it is better for them to worship God.

The truth of the matter is, a child has trouble worshiping in a service planned for adults. Children whose legs dangle over an adult-size pew without the comfort of a backrest (think of yourself perched on a table for an hour) feel better on small chairs. Active minds mystified by the pastor's message can respond better to an illustrated story from the life of Christ. Enthusiastic singers unable to use a hymnal can praise God in songs chosen for the young.

But, you may ask, given children's immature development, their short attention spans, and difficulty with abstract ideas, should we really expect them to worship at all? Isn't worship largely an intellectual activity too demanding for children's young minds? Jesus did not think so. In answer to the Pharisee's rebuke for accepting the worship of children at the temple, Jesus referred to Psalm 8:2. ". . .have ye never read, Out of the mouths of babes and sucklings thou hast perfected praise?" (Matt. 21:16). Worshiping God was something Jesus expected children to be able to do.

If we have seen little evidence of children's worshiping in the past, perhaps that is because church programs have not been conducive to their worship. If we have trouble believing children have the necessary capacities for true worship, perhaps we need to examine what we mean by worship. Can we define clearly what "adult" worship is? One writer has suggested that it is because we have not examined the meaning of worship ourselves that we do not value it more highly for our children.[1]

Defining Worship

R. A. Torrey defined *worship* as "The specific act of

adoring contemplation of God." The word itself derives from the Anglo-Saxon *weorthscipe*, which later became worthship, and then worship. It means *to attribute worth to an object*.[2] We say, "Bill worships his money," or his car, or his golf clubs. When we observe, "Debbie worships her older sister," we mean she considers her sister someone deserving special esteem and respect. In this sense, worship includes and goes beyond love and adoration.

The biblical terms for worship imply a bowing down, the devoted attention of a servant to a kind master. The worshiper is above all aware of God's presence, even overwhelmed by it; he responds with a sense of reverence and delight. One young woman described it this way: "My soul doth magnify the Lord, And my spirit hath rejoiced in God my Saviour" (Luke 1:46-47). In other words, worship is a response of the emotions to the presence of One who is preeminently loved and admired.

We are led to worship as we contemplate the nature and works of God through studying His Word, observing His handiwork, praying and hearing His praises sung. The *forms* of worship—adoration, praise, thanksgiving—should be distinguished from the *means* of worship—quiet music, soaring architecture, inspiring words, glorious scenery. The latter can lead us to worship, but, as Grace McGavran points out, "For response...to become worship, it must be response to God, not just to beauty, to nature, or to anything besides God Himself."[3]

It is possible to perform the rites of worship without having God as our object. Jesus said to the Samaritan woman, "Ye worship ye know not what: we know what we worship: for salvation is of the Jews" (John 4:22). However, it was not Samaritan worship exclusively that drew Jesus' criticism. He frequently challenged the practice of Jews who laid more stress on the means of worship than on the feelings that motivated it. While Jesus participated regularly in temple worship, He was not always happy with traditional practices. He examined worshipers' motives for sacrifice (cleansing the temple), stewardship (the widow's mite), prayer (the Pharisee and the publican), and hearing the Word ("Search the scriptures. . ."). He taught that worship emanated from a lofty view of God. He reminded us that God is a Spirit, both the Source and Focus of all true worship. As He reveals Himself through His creation and especially through His Word, we worship Him in spirit and in truth.

Worshipers by Nature

When Jesus repeated the psalmist's claim that praise is perfected in children, he was confirming a characteristic observed in children everywhere: they are natural worshipers. Young children, especially, have an inbuilt sense of wonder, an amazement at the mysteries of life and the marvels of the created world. They readily perceive what C. S. Lewis celebrated in his writings as *the numinous* —a consciousness of the Holy—and what Frederick Faber remembered in "The God of My Childhood" as a "strangely pleasant fear." Children manifest far more readily than do their parents, a reverential sensitivity to the awesomeness of God.

In later childhood years this sense of wonder diminishes somewhat as nine- and ten-year-olds become more matter-of-fact about life in general. Older children are more often led to worship as they see God's mighty workings through ideal individuals, particularly Jesus, the powerful, miracle-working Savior.

Like the woman of Samaria, children may sometimes worship "they know not what." They may confuse the magical with the supernatural. Because they have not developed the mental understandings of adults, they must be led wisely into knowledgeable worship. Christian parents can accomplish this through family worship. They can also take advantage of those spontaneous experiences when a child's heart is caught up in the bright flight of a butterfly or the warm embrace of father's goodnight. In these moments a child will sincerely praise God with his parent's guidance. In the church we have a full hour every week when we can plan specific opportunities for children's worship and create an atmosphere in which it can occur. During this church-time hour, as children come to recognize the Son of God, as they are led to new understandings of His nature and work, they too can worship Him in spirit and in truth.

Three-year-old Keith and his mother had spent a happy morning together, enjoying a holiday from nursery school and teaching. They worked outdoors, did a craft project, and talked about how good God was to give us days like this. At noon Mother made Keith's favorite lunch and asked him to pray. This is what he said: "Dear God, thank you for the beautiful day. Thank you for this wonderful food. And thank you for the wonderful life we've been having. Amen."

Children and Worship in Bible Days

If Christians today are concerned about the spiritual growth of their children, it is because the Bible taught them to be. Both Old and New Testaments specify what the attitude of God's people should be toward the growing generation.

William Barclay says of the religious training of children in Bible days, "No nation has ever set the child more deliberately in the midst than the Jews did."[4] The Jew was sure that of all people the child was dearest to God. Biblical scholars of the day taught that the almond blossoms on the gold candlesticks of the temple represented "the children who learn in school." The Talmud declared that, "So long as there are children in the schools Israel's enemies cannot prevail against her."

Worship of Yahweh was an integral part of the Hebrew child's life. As soon as he could speak, he was taught to recite morning and evening the Shema of Deuteronomy 6:4, "Hear, O Israel: The Lord our God is one Lord." When the child was old enough to ride on his father's shoulders, he was brought to the Feast of Tabernacles. At age three he began going with his father to regular worship at the synagogue. While children were not liable to keep the many Sabbath laws, their fathers were responsible to see that they observed Sabbath worship.

The mandate of Deuteronomy 6 made religious instruction the direct responsibility of parents. Children were to see holiness in their parents' lives, and they were to hear the Word of God from their lips, not only in times of formal instruction but in the routine activities of life: "when thou walkest by the way, and when thou liest down, and when thou risest up" (Deut. 6:7). Moreover, God's testimonies and statutes were to be deliberately visualized on the doorposts and gates of Hebrew homes in order to incite children to ask questions about their meaning (Deut. 6:8-9, 20). Before there ever was a school to teach him, a son would learn from his father the history of his country, the holy righteousness of God, the bounty of God in the world of nature.

That children were to be active participants in the festivals and temple worship is evident in the Scriptures. Psalm 78 testifies to the people's zeal to inspire worship of the Lord in the hearts of their children, "shewing to the generation to come the praises of the Lord, and his strength, and his wonderful works that he hath done" (v. 4). Psalm 148, that great litany of praise, clearly invites children to join their parents in worship of the Creator: "Both young men, and maidens; old men, and children: Let them praise the name of the Lord: for his name alone is excellent" (vv. 12-13).

Nehemiah painted a vivid picture of the revival in Judah, when "men and women, and all that could hear with understanding" (Neh. 8:2)—the Jerusalem Bible makes that simply "children"—were brought together in the street near Jerusalem's watergate to see the sacred books opened and hear the words of the Law. At the dedication of the wall of Jerusalem's Watergate to see the sacred books opened and for God had made them rejoice with great joy: the wives also and the children rejoiced: so that the joy of Jerusalem was heard even afar off" (Neh. 12:43).

In Israel's early history religious instruction centered in the home, the land, and the festivals of the Hebrew year. When the Exile in Babylon severed worship from Jerusalem and the temple, the survival of Judaism came to depend as never before upon educating the next generation. As a result, during the captivity and after the return to Judah, teaching and worship both became centered in the local synagogue. By the first century A.D., when the gospels were being written, Jerusalem was said to have had 480 synagogues, each one with a school. In the days of Jesus, Jewish education was widespread: the New Testament period would be the age of widest literacy for 1,800 years to come.[5]

After Ezra's reform, the curriculum in Hebrew schools became formalized. Reading, writing, and memorization of Scripture were paramount. Certain Bible passages were considered basic to every child's religious education. Significantly, the first passages listed for the child to learn had to do with worship. Children were to learn the Hallel—passages from the psalms of praise, 113-118. Children were also expected to know the story of Creation, Genesis 1-5, and the essence of the Levitical Law, Leviticus 1-8.

Memorization was the most common teaching technique although children were sometimes given little parchment scrolls containing essential Scripture passages. On his first day of school a child received a personal Scripture text—a verse which began with the first letter of his name and ended with the last letter.

Of those who taught children, the highest standards were expected. Jews honored their teachers and considered their calling an important one. A current saying held that it was "as great a privilege to teach a child the Law, as it was to receive it on Mount Sinai from the hands of God."[6] In the faithfulness and skill of synagogue teachers lay the preservation of Jewish faith and culture. "If you would destroy the Jews," says the Talmud, "you must first destroy their teachers."

The New Testament writer James, whose epistle clearly reflected his Jewish background, reminded Christians that the teacher's task is not to be taken lightly: "Let not many of you become teachers, my brethren, knowing that as such we shall incur a stricter judgment" (James 3:1 NASB). James's words are similar in spirit to those of his elder brother, who spoke severely of adults' responsibility to nurture children's faith. He said that anyone who put a stumblingblock in the way of a believing child would be better off drowned. One often wonders, watching listless children yawn through Sunday school and church, if shoddy teaching, meager facilities, and incomprehensible language were not among the stumblingblocks which Jesus had in mind.

Jesus and Children

This age needs to reexamine Jesus' attitude toward

children. The familiar biblical vignettes of Jesus and children have become so encrusted with traditions that the events themselves are obscured. Moments in Jesus' ministry which should flash with meaning are too often frozen in images from Victorian literature and sentimental pictures. We need to strip away the ideas we have accumulated and examine anew what the events reveal about Jesus and the children whose lives He touched.

We need to listen to His teaching about children. Jesus spoke to a world startlingly like our own in its mistreatment of the young. In the Mediterranean society of the first century child abuse was endemic. Greek and Roman parents practiced abortion and infanticide as a matter of course. Wealthy Greeks disposed of unwanted children in order to keep the family inheritance intact. Poor families sold children into slavery and prostitution; sometimes they deliberately maimed a child to make him a more effective beggar. These practices at times threatened the growth of the population. During the years of the Pax Romana, government officials expressed concern because parents reared so few of their offspring.

The Jews of that time were unique in prizing children as evidences of God's favor. The psalmist's words lay deep in the national consciousness: "Lo, children are an heritage of the Lord: and the fruit of the womb is his reward. As arrows are in the hand of a mighty man; so are children...Happy is the man that hath his quiver full of them" (Ps. 127:3-5). The Jews showed concern for nurturing and educating the young. Jesus' attitude toward children reflected that of the larger Jewish society, but included also his regard for children's faith as a model for adults.

Jesus Knew Children

By His words and actions Jesus showed a sensitive

concern for children and an intimate knowledge of their lives. His example shaped the attitude of the church in its historic commitment to the welfare of the young.

There are almost one hundred direct references to children in the New Testament; 75 percent of these are in the first three gospels. We will consider the most prominent of the gospel passages individually, but we should refer at least briefly to those scattered throughout the Acts and epistles. The early church had no specific program for children, nor were special doctrines established concerning them. The children of Christians were, however, clearly considered part of the worshiping community. Wives and children accompanied the men who bid farewell to Paul as he left Tyre on his trip to Jerusalem (Acts 21:5). The Philippian jailer's family received Christ along with him and were baptized (Acts 16:32-34). Children were urged to obey their parents in order to please Christ (Col. 3:20), and parents were advised (long before psychologists taught the value of positive reinforcement) not to discourage their children by constant criticism, but instead to nurture and teach them in the Lord (Eph. 6:4).

Jesus and Children in the Gospels

We tend to picture the Man Jesus most often in His preaching and teaching roles, removed somewhat from the hurly-burly of everyday family life. We forget that as the elder brother of a large family He grew up caring for (and possibly "parenting," if Joseph died in Jesus' youth as many believe) several younger siblings, intervening in their squabbles, drying their tears, teaching them to handle tools, rounding them up when play took them too far from home.

Throughout their records of His ministry, Matthew, Mark, and Luke show Jesus singling children out of the throng, deliberately giving them attention, indicating by His conversation that He was aware of their activities. Luke especially reveals Jesus' interest in children. He watched their games in the marketplace (Luke 7:32), knew how they prized gifts from their fathers (Luke 11:13), pictured them rolled up in bed at night with their parents in the manner of a Mideastern family of that day (Luke 11:7). Predicting the fall of Jerusalem, Jesus expressed compassion for the women and nursing children who would suffer in the deportation. Treading to His Crucifixion, He told the grieving women of the city to weep instead for themselves and their children in the cruel days that lay ahead.

Jesus' choice of words sometimes disclosed His affinity for the experiences of childhood. Early in His ministry He had taught His disciples to use Abba, the child's word for Father, when addressing God, a term considered much too intimate by the theologians of the day. Again, in the final hour of His agony He cried out to His Father in the words from Psalms taught to every Jewish child as an evening prayer: "Into thy hands I commend my spirit" (Luke 23:46).

It is not enough to stand above a child and tell him how he ought to live. Adults who would minister to children must remember how it feels to be a child. Jesus remembered.

Jesus Accepted Children's Worship

It was a day of unprecedented events in Jerusalem. Those who saw it never would forget. Children, especially, would recall in later years the kingly man on the small donkey, the noisy parade, the awesome authority of Jesus as He cleared the temple of sheep, pigeons, goats, and moneychangers. They would feel forever the electrifying effect of His miracles—the blind eyes seeing, the lame legs running.

To the young boys milling about in the temple that Palm Sunday—many attending with their fathers, others there as choirboys for Passover services—Jesus could be no other than the mighty Son of David, the Messiah they had been taught to expect. He fit the image of a Deliverer, and they hailed Him in glad recognition while older and more sophisticated minds explained Him away.

To Jesus, the children's cheers must have been a welcome contrast to the harping criticism of Jerusalem's learned rulers. *The Interpreter's Bible* comments on this passage that Jesus drew strength from the children's love. More than thirty years earlier, He had struggled into human history as an insignificant peasant's child, unnoticed except by angels; now, in His triumphal entry, it must have meant something to Him to be hailed by children such as He once was: "Hosanna to the Son of David!" He accepted their worship as an indication of true faith—a quality He seemed to prize above all others. Defending their unrestrained adoration, Jesus quoted the Septuagint version of the Scripture mentioned earlier, "Out of the mouths of babes and sucklings thou hast perfected praise." Far from being blasphemous, their worship *furnished completely* (perfected) the praise due to the Son of God.

Before the week was out Jesus would be challenged by a harrassing lawyer to name the greatest commandment. The law He chose in response was one that even children can obey: "Thou shalt love the Lord thy God with all thy heart, and with all thy soul, and with all thy mind" (Matt. 22:37). Whatever a person's capacities are, he can love the Lord with all the heart and soul and mind he has—at age five, or eleven, or thirty-five. Had we written the law we might have mentioned the mind first, considering mental ability of primary importance to belief, but Jesus put it last after the seat of the emotions. This is consistent with the differences in the way children and adults respond. In adults, knowledge and reason most often lead to faith; in children, whose mental powers are undeveloped, emotion more readily leads to faith. A child will not understand the intricacies of revelation and essential doctrines, but he can love God with all the heart and mind his developmental level will allow. To Jesus, this is acceptable worship.

Jesus Was Accessible to Children

Our son came home from the campus of a nearby Christian college one evening and said, "I talked to Dr. Bailey about my credits this afternoon."

"Dr. Bailey? You went to PRESIDENT Bailey about your credits?"

"Sure. Why not?"

"Because the president of a college is too busy to talk with individual students about their credits. You bother someone else about it!"

"But I knew he'd talk to me, Mom. Dr. Bailey always has time for me."

Right or wrong, our son felt that he had a special relationship with a very important person, and that person honored his faith.

Children seemed to know instinctively that they had special entree to Jesus. When crowds and schedules pressed, when His friends tried to protect Him, when adults wanted Him to be busy with more important things, children had prior claim to His attention. He interrupted a sermon to go with a father to the deathbed of his little girl; as a curious crowd gathered, He hurried to deliver a lunatic boy from demons. Just back from a preaching tour, He stopped on the streets of Capernaum to heal a nobleman's son. Pagan children mattered, too; He healed the Syrophoenician's daughter. Martyn White points out that the four children Jesus healed were Jewish and Gentile, two boys and two girls, two from wealthy families, and two from ordinary or poor ones.[8] He was available to all kinds of children—too available, His disciples felt, on at least one well-known occasion.

Most of us give prominent place to this occasion on the mental mural we all carry of Jesus' life and ministry. It is recorded in all three synoptic Gospels; Mark, usually so terse, described the scene most fully (Mark 10:13-16). Jesus was preaching on vital subjects of great interest to His audience: matters of marriage and divorce, riches and renunciation, publicans and Pharisees. Suddenly the discussion was interrupted by a somewhat noisy and undignified group—village mothers coming with their children to ask Jesus to bless them. The disciples briskly headed them off. But Jesus, sizing up the matter, was angry with His disciples (Mark said He was "much displeased," the only time that harsh word was used of Jesus) and called the children back.

One commentator observes, "If we wish to know what Jesus cared deeply about one sure clue is to be found in the things that aroused His indignation."[9] He was angry with the Pharisees who cared more for Sabbath law than for relieving human suffering; now He was angry with His followers' insensitivity to the needs and feelings of the young and powerless.

"Let the children come," He said. "Allow them, do not forbid, do not prevent them from coming to me." Jesus' words implied that He knew the children wanted to come and would come to Him if they were not prevented. This provides an important insight into Jesus' understanding of children's spiritual readiness: He indicated that children, unlike adults, would come to Him *if they were not hindered.* This quality of readiness He considered something that should be cherished and encouraged.

By their implicit trust in His availability, children fulfill the prerequisite for pleasing God spoken of in Hebrews 11:6, "He that cometh to God must believe that he is, and that he is a rewarder of them that diligently seek him."

How well children meet this criterion was brought home to me a few years ago when my ten-year-old daughter told me how much she loved this verse. She could not then explain why, but later, with the superior reasoning power of a thirteen-year-old, analyzed her feelings. "I knew I believed that God was, and that He would help me to know Him if I asked Him. This verse convinced me that God accepted my faith, so I knew everything was right between us." Adults have to learn that "the All-holy is the All-gracious";[10] children seem to know it instinctively. They come to Jesus with the confidence of one who knows he is in the presence of a greater, more deserving, but kindly disposed person.

Children in the long-ago streets of Palestine knew that Jesus was accessible to them. They were confident of His favor, not because of who they were, but because of who Jesus was. That is why Jesus used them as examples of the humility necessary to enter the kingdom. Adults can learn from children to ". . .draw near with a true heart in full assurance of faith" (Heb. 10:22).

Jesus Expressed His Love for Children

If the last hundred years of child study, research, analysis, and theorizing have taught us anything definitive about children, it is that they require much affection. Children deprived of the warmth of caring adults suffer lasting psychological damage. Psychologists, teachers, and parents know that children need physical contact with people who love them. They need hugs, pats, smiles, and horseplay. They need grandfather's knees for bouncing and father's shoulders for riding on. They need to hug mom and have her hug back.

Affection was Jesus' natural way with children. In the brief scene described in Mark 9:35-37 we see evidence of this. Jesus called a young child (Peter's son?) to join Him as He talked with His disciples. He then encircled the boy in His arms, as if to make him comfortable, before proceeding to give the disciples a lesson in humility.

On other occasions we see Him helping, touching, reaching out to the children He encountered. To raise Jairus's daughter He took her small, lifeless hand in His; to lift the lunatic boy lying corpse-like on the ground Jesus stooped, took him by the hand, and helped him up.

Far from the reserved, impassive figure some would make Him, Jesus by His manner with children was seen to be warm and fatherly. Many a preacher having to interrupt his sermon to bless a group of children might simply place his hands on them and let them go. What Jesus did, Mark tells us, was to take each child in His arms, lay His hands on him and give him His blessing. Although He did not need to pick them up, He seemed to want to demonstrate His love for each one. It was this manifest affection that endeared Jesus to children, that caused every instance of their being together to be marked by instant rapport. His eyes and arms, as well as His words, told them that He loved them.

Jesus Instructed the Church about Children

Nothing that we have said about Jesus and children should lead us to infer that He considered them sinless. It is easy to get sentimental about children. God has made them (perhaps for their protection) both beautiful and lovable. That does not mean, however, that we should idealize their charm and spontaneity or confuse naivete' with innocence.

Those who know children best do not make that mistake.

Jesus knew that children were prone to temptation and sin, as all humans are. He spoke of the danger of their being led astray. We search in vain, however, for any instance of Jesus' rebuking or correcting a child. Nor do we know of any time when He specifically called children to repentance. What He did instead was to make His Church responsible for their welfare and spiritual nurture. In the longest passage in the Bible concerning Jesus and children, Matthew records Jesus' charge to the Church to protect and guide the young (Matt. 18:1-14).

We are familiar with the circumstances surrounding this event. Jesus and His disciples were resting in a home in Capernaum, probably Peter's. Earlier in the day the disciples had had an argument over leadership. Jesus wanted to discuss it with them. (It could sound from Matthew's account as though the disciples opened the discussion, but we know from the other evangelists that they were reluctant at first to talk about the incident—Jesus had to probe.) Jesus centered the discussion around a child, a flesh-and-blood example of the kind of humility and teachableness that Jesus wanted the disciples to emulate. He made clear to them that God is no respecter of persons: any child in the kingdom is as important as they are. In the course of the conversation Jesus outlined the Church's duty to children.

1. Every child is to be received as though he were Jesus Himself (v. 5).
2. So important is a child's growth that anyone causing a child to stumble (the meaning of offend) would be better off collared with a millstone and thrown in the sea (v. 6).
3. The child's world will be full of stumblingblocks; Christians are not to be among them (v. 7).

4. Jesus' followers are personally responsible to rid themselves of any offending habit or bad example, however painful or inconvenient that might be (vv. 8-9).
5. No one is to look down upon (the Greek word means despise, disdain, think little or nothing of) these little ones; they have a special place in the Father's heart (v. 10).

After illustrating with the story of the shepherd concerned for his lost sheep, Jesus summed up His teaching about children: it is against the will of God for any child to be allowed to perish. By example and nurture, therefore, the Church is to guide the young safely into the fold.

This passage makes clear that Jesus considered childhood a pivotal time, one in which spiritual direction may be irrevocably decided. We can also conclude from these and other of Jesus' statements that there is much in a child's nature that makes it easy for him, during his early years, to trust in Christ. In verse 6 He speaks of "these little ones which believe in me." Children can and do believe, but they may also go astray through the neglect and bad example of adults. The church must do everything in its power to see that the child is nurtured to a mature faith in Christ, to so lead him during his years of trust that he will never fall into unbelief.

The word Jesus uses for stumblingblock—*scandalizo*, occasions of sin—refers to those who endanger the salvation of others. To the Jews, causing someone to lose his faith was the most serious of sins. Jeroboam was remembered in infamy as the one "who caused Israel to sin." Jesus went on record as considering it a crime not unlike one that would be punished by execution. In the years following His death and Resurrection the early church would take this passage seriously enough to include children in the benefits of worship and fellowship, and to make care of orphans a special enterprise.

Has the church since that time taken Jesus' words as seriously? Some would argue that it has not. Church buildings and budgets have not always reflected the centrality of children's spiritual needs. Until very recent years little room was made for children in the provisions for worship and fellowship. Part of the reason children's work has been given lower priority than other church ministries may lie in the traditional interpretation of the key passage in Matthew 18. Commentators by and large have maintained that Jesus was referring in this passage not to children but to those who are young in the faith—that Jesus was talking about discipleship rather than child nurture.

Such an interpretation is bound to blunt the effect of Jesus' words as far as children are concerned. Interestingly enough, in Mark's rendition of this episode, we see John the disciple taking the same exegetical direction and being corrected. He interrupted Jesus' discourse to ask a question about accepting one who works miracles in Jesus' name, but "followeth not us" (Mark 9:38). John's question seemed to be, "Should we accept this person as a new disciple?" Like the great Teacher that He was, Jesus responded briefly to John's question, then returned the conversation to the subject—their responsibility to protect and nurture children's faith (Mark 9:42).

The gospel records show that children occupied a central place in Jesus' concern for mankind; He made them a special focus of His attention, His miracles, and His teaching. He welcomed and commended their worship. He modeled for us the kind of affection and regard we should express in our relationships with them.

If we accept at face value the words of Jesus in Matthew 18:1-14 as referring to children specifically (though principles may certainly apply to others as well), we must conclude that Jesus made the growth and development of children's faith a priority concern of the Church, on a level with evangelism. Churches that relegate children's ministries to a low level of priority do so against the expressed will of Jesus. We need to reevaluate our programs to see if we are receiving children as we would receive Jesus Himself.

Notes

1. Eleanor Hance, "Teaching Children to Worship and Pray," *Childhood Education in the Church*, eds. R. Zuck and R. E. Clark (Chicago: Moody Press, 1974), p. 27.

2. Ralph P. Martin, *Worship in the Early Church* (London: Marshall, Mayor and Scott, 1964), p. 10.

3. Grace McGavran, *Learning How Children Worship* (St. Louis: Bethany, 1964), p. 11.

4. William Barclay, *Train up a Child, Educational Ideals in the Ancient World* (Grand Rapids: Baker Book House, 1974), p. 9.

5. Ibid., p. 14.

6. Ibid., p. 43.

7. Ibid., p. 267.

8. Martyn White, "Love Relationship," *Spotcast*, Spring 1977, p. 1.

9. *The Interpreter's Bible* (Nashville: Abingdon Press, 1979), p. 799.

10. Martin, *Worship*, p. 13.

2

How a Child Learns: According to His Way

The distracted father almost wept as he spoke: "I don't understand it. We've brought our children up to love God and honor His Word. They've known nothing but Christian love and discipline since they were babies. Now, here is my sixteen-year-old daughter, pregnant and unmarried. What happened to God's promise? We trained our daughter in the way she should go—why did she depart from it?"

We have heard Proverbs 22:6 all our Christian lives. When our experience confirms it we rejoice; when it does not, we hurt and wonder. Many a broken-hearted parent has asked God why? why? why? after a Christian upbringing and church education, an adolescent or adult child has departed from the way. They feel betrayed—by their children, and, sometimes, by God.

It is possible that we have interpreted as a promise what the inspired writer meant as sage advice. It is also possible, however, that the familiar translations of this proverb have not served us well as parents and teachers. We might be enlightened to consider alternative renderings of the Hebrew words. The sense of the King James Version is to emphasize the *content* of instruction at the expense of the *process*; several other trustworthy translations emphasize the process of teaching the child as well as the content of the instruction. Hebrew scholars, Keil and Delitzsche, illuminate the passage by their rendering "Give to the child instruction conformable to his way, so he will not, when he is old, depart from it."[1] In the same spirit the Berkeley Modern English Bible says, "Educate a child according to his life requirements..."[2] and the Jerusalem Bible notes the possible meaning, "according to his dispositions."[3] The Expositor's Bible translates the phrase "according to his way,"[4] and Matthew Henry, "according as he is capable."[5] These renderings are consistent with what we know of the child's manner of learning: he must be given truth in ways that make it possible for him to receive it. Just as the infant must be fed milk and not meat because milk is a form of nourishment suited to his development, so spiritual nourishment for the young must be suited to youthful capabilities.

In his book, *A Theology of Christian Education,* Lawrence O. Richards alerts us to Delitzsche's century-old but valid commentary on Proverbs 22:6. "The instruction of youth...ought to be conformed to the nature of youth,... The manner of instruction ought to regulate itself according to the stage of life and its peculiarities; the method ought to be arranged according to the degree of development which the mental and bodily life of the youth has arrived at."[6]

A closer look at the expression, "Train up" may also improve our understanding of the process of instruction. Early Christians translated the Hebrew word *catechizatio.* It means literally *to put in the mouth,* to affect the taste, or the palate, as when a nurse would put date syrup in the mouth of an infant. In other words, instruction for the child must be both nourishing and palatable.

The picture that emerges from a careful study of the verse is not one of adult trainers placing a child permanently on a road marked Righteousness, but one of caring adults nurturing the child with truth he needs and can receive at his age.

The Child's Development

In recent decades psychologists and educators, searching for a better understanding of children's thinking and development, have conducted massive amounts of research with children all over the world. Their studies have significance for Christian teachers and parents. What the research uncovered indicates that children everywhere go through discernable stages of intellectual and moral development, just as they go through stages of physical development.

Children sit up before they stand; they crawl before they walk; they cut their front teeth before their molars. We can confidently predict this progression in growth and would not be so foolish as to try to coax a three-month-old to walk or to expect a child's first utterance to be a compound sentence. We know that much as we may cajole, encourage, or assist baby to walk, he will not take a step until his fat little legs can take the pressure and his nervous system can provide the proper motor control.

Intellectual stages of development are less familiar to us than are physical stages, but researchers tell us they are almost as predictable. Development powerfully influences learning and behavior. The better we understand how children at different stages think and learn, the better will be the learning and worship experiences we plan for them.

How Children Think and Feel

Although human emotional needs are constant throughout life, intellectual processes change with development. One thing research in child development has made very clear is that children are more like adults emotionally than either physically or intellectually. Human beings seem to begin life with a full range of emotional responses, but only a starter set of intellectual ones. As a result, children are a great deal like adults in their *feelings,* but very different from adults in their *thinking.*

We sometimes act as though the opposite were true: we expect children to think deeply but not to feel deeply. Teachers often speak to children in a tone of voice they would never use with their peers. We feel free to criticize a child's work publicly when we would afford privacy to an adult; we talk about children in their hearing as though not expecting them to be embarrassed. On the other hand, we are surprised when they do not think as we do. We use abstract expressions familiar to us but obscure to them (the Word of God, the Lord is my Shepherd), and expect children to understand that those words do not mean concretely what they say.

Since children are emotionally perceptive, we should assume that what would hurt or offend an adult would also hurt or offend a child. But because they are intellectually undeveloped, it is never safe to assume they understand a concept familiar to adults. I was reminded of this not long ago when I repeatedly used the expression, "the Word of God," in a lesson for primaries. One of our brighter third graders kept asking me, "What is the Word of God, what *is* it?" Finally I held up my Bible. "Why, you know, John—*this* is God's Word." "I know, I know," he insisted, his blue eyes incredulous at my stupidity, "but what's *the word,* what's THE WORD?" I finally understood that John thought there was, literally, one particular word which was God's word! Not unreasonably, he wondered why a church teacher of my vintage could not come up with it. I knew John spoke for scores of other children I had unwittingly confused with that concept.

The Child's Brain—A Growing Organ

The problem is not simply that young children have not had enough experience to understand abstract ideas. There are also physical reasons they cannot perform the mental operations necessary to handle such concepts. The infant's brain at birth is a potential rather than a completed human brain. Many functions will not be possible until further growth has taken place within that remarkable organ. A process called myelination is especially important to the thinking function. In young children the nerve fibers along which impulses travel are largely uninsulated, causing thought processes to be relatively slow. During childhood and up to about age twenty the myelin sheath gradually encloses more and more nerve fibers, allowing thoughts to be conducted with greater speed. Brain scans show that not until the onset of adolescence, at about age twelve, do children's brains begin to show characteristic adult patterns of response.[7] It is no accident that since biblical times the twelfth and thirteenth years have often marked the young person's official participation in the life of the religious community. With physical maturity comes new ability to handle abstract ideas.

Nevertheless, we should never think of the young child's mind as passive or inadequate! On the contrary, the brain from birth is a highly active and aggressive organ, relentlessly searching out patterns and seeking information, ceaselessly learning and, as some research indicates, even growing as a result of its own activity. What we should understand about mental development is that at certain stages the child moves to new plateaus of cognitive ability. He is able to handle concepts and problems which a year earlier would have baffled him in spite of our best efforts. That is why the teacher's timing in planning subject matter is so important. Learning depends on *maturation* as well as *information.*

Age Differences

If we are to heed the advice of the writer of Proverbs to teach children according to their way, we must consider carefully the developmental differences in the groups of children that we teach. How is a child of seven different from a child of five or eight? Is he, indeed, significantly different at all? Churches that group all children together for the worship hour apparently do not think so. We would be wise to study our children more carefully with an eye to how their developmental changes affect learning.

Every year that a child lives he attains new thresholds. A four-year-old is a different kind of person from a five-year-old, and an eight-year-old is light years away from what he was at five. That does not mean children of different ages cannot play together and learn from each other; of course they can, and do. But we have greater success in our teaching when we accommodate the characteristic needs and abilities of each age. We then eliminate some discipline problems and increase the chances that our students will learn.

The years of childhood are usually divided into three general levels; infancy (age 0 to 2), preschool (age 2 to 6), and elementary school years (age 6 to 11). These are broad categories, subdivided in various ways for teaching purposes.

Infancy—the Foundational Years, Age 0 to 2

A three-week-old baby enters the church nursery for the first time. This marks a significant event, the beginning, we would hope, of a lifetime of participation in the local church. The newborn is already an individual, totally absorbed in his effort to organize the multitude of sensations, sounds, and images in the universe he represents. For the next two years his intellectual tasks will be profound: he must learn to distinguish the difference between himself and everything else he encounters; to learn that things which disappear from his view continue to exist; and, in his second year, learn that words and objects can stand for other realities.

Gradually the child learns that his mother is not a part of himself, that she does not cease to exist when she goes out the door, but can be expected to appear there again if he cries for her. Later he learns that *Daddy* means the larger person with the deeper voice who also holds him and cares for his needs. *From interaction with adults, or the painful lack of it, will come the basic sense of trust or mistrust which will color all his future relationships.*

The significance of this period for children in the church is twofold. (1) The child forms a positive attitude toward church and the people associated with it because of the warm, pleasant experiences he has had there. (2) The child's healthy development is promoted as church workers meet his needs and interact with him. Nursery volunteers sometimes underestimate their influence: What difference can I make in a few hours a week? Extensive studies of young children and their environments indicate, however, that though parents have by far the greatest influence on their young child, other adults who care for him regularly also leave their mark on his development. They are outstanding figures in the simple geography of his world.

Because of their potential impact, nursery workers must be thoughtfully chosen and thoroughly trained. They must know that caring adults are the most important factor in a child's development. The one stimulus that the infant responds to most often and most eagerly is a human face or voice. God has created in the child a need for human exchange; by his actions—smiling, crying, gazing, grasping—he constantly challenges others to interaction. One image above all others never fails to lock his gaze—a human face, or something that resembles a face. As early as six weeks of age the infant's eyes begin to rove, searching for another pair of human eyes on which to focus.[8] How important it is that as he looks up from a crib or carpeted floor in the church nursery, his gaze is met by eyes of love!

Early Childhood Years, Age 2 to 6

The two-year-old emerges from infancy at an unsteady trot, running, climbing, chattering, questioning, constantly testing his new powers, and, to the despair of his parents, asserting himself at every opportunity. At this age the child's thoughts derive from his actions; he literally must act upon information or experiences to learn about them. He acts, *then* he thinks!

Jean Piaget, the Swiss psychologist whose studies of children's thinking have won worldwide respect, has a great deal to say about the importance of the years between infancy and elementary school. During these four years the child makes great strides in cognitive as well as physical development, attaining astonishing facility in what Piaget calls the *symbolic function*—the use of an object to represent something else (a block can be a car, a stone can be a turtle) and the use of language to represent people and things. (*Kitty* means the furry, gray thing with the swift claws; *Bow-wow* means the larger fellow with the dripping tongue.) But the preschooler's steady flow of talk can be deceptive: he appears to know much more than he actually understands.

Piaget calls the young child's thinking *preoperational*; that is, while he is inquisitive and learning very rapidly, he cannot yet perform certain mental operations, or functions, necessary for logical thought. We can detect several distinctive features in the young child's way of thinking. We should keep them in mind as we choose learning content and activities for this age.

1. *The young child's thought is egocentric.* He can see things from only one point of view—his own. *Egocentrism* should not be confused with egotism, a thoroughly adult sin. It is rather a function of the child's limited perception, which is still oriented around himself. During infancy he learned to differentiate himself (in his own mind) from the rest of the world, but he has not overcome the belief that what *he* thinks and feels everyone else also thinks and feels! The preschooler speaks whatever comes into his mind because he believes other people are thinking that, too. He does not keep secrets well because he thinks everyone knows what he knows, anyway. He is surprised that Mommy cannot feel his stomachache, and in the same way, he is surprised that his playmate cries when he sinks his fingernails into her chubby arm. Because he feels no pain, he thinks there is no pain.

    Having neither great experience nor strong reasoning powers the preschooler is dominated by his perceptions, however false. He believes things are as they appear to be. The moon follows him when he travels (doesn't it appear to?), Daddy's head reaches to the ceiling (it seems to if you are looking up from the height of his knees), the toy truck teacher showed me is mine (since I'm using it). Plenty of experience with other children and patient guidance from adults, along with his normal developmental changes, help the growing preschooler begin to see things from other's viewpoints—a task many still find challenging in adulthood.

2. *The young child associates proximity with cause.* That is, if two things happen together, he assumes one caused the other. A child whose mother cries in his presence may feel he made her cry. One child thought raising the window shade made the sun come up. Every morning when she put the shade up, there was the sun! After a recent earthquake many young children refused to get into their beds the next night. Since the quake happened while they slept, they felt that being in bed had something to do with it. If you tell a story about something very sad happening to someone, expect preschoolers to think the person somehow was at fault.

3. *Preoperational children typically center on one aspect of an experience.* They do not see the larger picture, but focus on one, often insignificant detail which attracts and holds their attention. They cannot deal with several aspects of a situation at the same time. For this reason it is wise to keep pictures and stories simple and uncluttered, with colorful, clear, images and little extraneous detail. Even then, expect some misunderstanding. A four-year-old in our Sunday school became upset when a man with a beard walked into class. He insisted that the man was Jesus. We assured him otherwise, and it soon became apparent that he was the father of one of the children. Nevertheless, the boy could not be convinced. Days later when he encountered bearded men, he continued to ask if they were Jesus. He had centered on one feature and was not able to consider other evidence.

4. *The preschool child thinks intuitively rather than logically.* He feels his way through a problem; he does not reason through it. Instead of building one fact upon another as an older child does, the preschooler freely associates elements of different experiences which may not have any logical connection. For this reason chronology has no importance for him, and he is vague about time in general —Jesus may have lived when Grandma was a girl. Bible content for children this age should appeal to the child's feelings rather than to his intellect. Jesus is our Friend. God is our Loving Father who watches over us day and night, who gives us grown-ups to care for us and a home to live in. Prayers should be simple and closely related to the child's everyday life. Teaching and recall of Scripture, too, should be tied to the child's needs and experiences.

   Only at seven or eight, when they have reached a new intellectual plateau, can children conceptualize well enough to understand scriptural teachings like the Ten Commandments and the Lord's Prayer. Although they may have been taught to parrot the words earlier, we should not deceive ourselves into thinking they have learned on a meaningful level.

5. *The young child adapts new information to fit into his mental structure, often distorting it in the process.* Illustrations of this characteristic are legion—teachers love to swap them over coffee. Two well-worn examples are children's misinterpretation of an old hymn, "Gladly, the cross-eyed bear," and their way of saying the Pledge of Allegience—"to the Republic for Richard Stans...." Delightful though these mental misconstructions are,

we need to take them seriously. They tell us something of children's struggle to make sense out of the incomprehensible language they too often encounter. The primary boy who prayed, "Deliver us from eagles" was distorting the abstract word *evil* into something he could understand wanting to be delivered from!

The fact that we deal with some biblical images which are not part of twentieth century life should make us extra cautious. One little girl confounded her teacher by asking if Jesus barked. The teacher had said Jesus was the Good Shepherd, and the only shepherd that little girl knew anything about was the family watchdog—a German Shepherd, hardly the image the teacher was hoping to convey. A more knowledgeable child might know what a shepherd is, but believe Jesus actually herded sheep—not a serious distortion, perhaps, but inaccurate just the same.

Our worst mistake is to think we can clarify a difficult concept for children by using an object lesson or analogy to illustrate it. These may do more harm than good. One visual aid on the market seeks to teach the concept of the Trinity to children by using the three parts of an apple—peel (Father), flesh (Son), and core (Spirit). But as the little girl and her watchdog show, young children do not grasp complex ideas by comparing them to simple objects; instead they *reduce or distort* the abstract concept to fit the familiar object. Thus God has three parts like an apple, so Jesus must be the best "part" of God, since we enjoy the flesh of the apple and throw the rest away.

On those rare occasions (with young children) when our teaching touches a doctrine as abstract as the Trinity, we will teach with more integrity and less confusion to the child by simply stating the truth without trying to illustrate it: the Father is God, Jesus the Son is God, the Holy Spirit is God; and although we do not understand this, we know it to be true. Elaboration and analogies should await higher mental functioning. With children at this level of development, illustrations meant to clarify merely mystify.

Advantages of Teaching in Early Childhood

While we have focused on the limitations of the preschooler's mental development, these should not discourage us from teaching and worshiping with this age. Far from it! Anyone who has joined in a nursery child's spontaneous prayer or observed a group of two-year-olds clap and sway around the record player, totally involved in a song of praise, knows they are as open to God's leading as any adult. There are great rewards in helping them to worship. In addition to the child's natural sense of wonder discussed in the first chapter of this book, there are other important reasons for providing teaching and worship experiences for children this age.

1. *The young child is more responsive to the loving overtures of adults than he will be at any time in his life.* If our teaching must be short on instruction it can be long on influence! Although it takes many experiences for a preschooler to develop a relationship with an adult, once it is secure the relationship can be strategic. By smiles, hugs, and eye contact the teacher can nourish the child emotionally. At a later age the child will still need affection, but will not be able to accept it as freely. During the preschool years we have opportunity to get in on the ground floor of a child's development and predispose him, by our love, to receive God's love.

    Dr. Ross Campbell in his wise and practical book, *How to Really Love Your Child,* advises teachers of this age group to watch for the child who shows emotional deprivation. This usually reveals itself in the child's failure to make eye contact, in his reluctance to speak, and in his manner of approaching the teacher sideways—or even backwards! Campbell advises the teacher to help this child by (1) teaching him while sitting across the table from him, (2) holding him, (3) making eye contact with him, as much as he can tolerate.[9] These acts of positive love, Campbell explains, fill his emotional tank and free him to love others in turn.

Whenever they have behaved badly, children especially need to feel our unconditional love. Seek out the child you have had to discipline. In a natural, unforced way, let him know that while he lost your approval, he did not lose your love. This will help him learn to seek and accept God's forgiveness.

2. *Young children copy the actions of teachers and parents.* Boys and girls alike play Mommy and Daddy; they fix supper and fill the car with gas; they "spank" baby brother, gossip on the phone, pray before eating, dress up for church—mimicking all the worthy and unworthy behaviors they observe in adult models. For the child, dramatic play is a means of incorporating information into his system. For the teacher, it can provide helpful insight into learning. Teachers and parents who model Christian behaviors for the child to incorporate are teaching in the best possible way for this age.

Bible stories, too, can provide models of people who acted in ways pleasing to God and helpful to others. Miriam cared for her baby brother; a poor woman shared what she had with God's servant, Elijah; Jesus healed the sick and suffering; Peter and John stopped to help a lame man walk.

In a child's learning of Bible stories, teachers sometimes notice a characteristic called *deferred imitation*—acting out at a later time something the child seemed to forget. One five-year-old surprised his teacher by building a boat in the block corner and acting out Jesus' miraculous haul of fish months after he had heard the story. In the child's way he was assimilating the story by imitating it.

3. *Young children believe what they are told.* During these years children impute infinite wisdom to adults and older children. "My daddy can fix it," the preschooler says of the hopelessly shattered vase. "My mommy told me!" she protests, defending her faith in the Easter Bunny. The preschooler believes that rules are right and should be obeyed because adults or older children made them up. He may find it impossible to obey the rules, but he has implicit faith that they are right.

It is easy, and unfortunately common, for people to take advantage of children's credulity. The older schoolmate's threat, "Let me have that swing or I'll report you to the principal," is a familiar ruse that invariably unseats the kindergartener. "Be quiet or the policeman will arrest you," or "Keep sticking your tongue out and your face will freeze that way," are effective comments because children believe them, but they backfire when the child himself learns to "misinform."

Because children will believe what we tell them about God, we must be careful always to represent Him truly. When teachers say things like, "God wants boys and girls to sit up nice and straight in church," they are making an assumption that may serve the cause of discipline, but does not honestly reflect God's nature. More than likely, He wants teachers to let them wiggle often. The same is true of Bible stories. If we have to modify a Bible story greatly in order to use it for preschoolers, we should save it for a later time.

In our hurry to instruct and "cover more of the Bible" we forget that preschool children do not need a new Bible story every week. They can benefit from learning the many ways one Bible story teaches us about God and how He wants us to live every day. Young children love repetition and delight to hear familiar stories again and again. After learning about Abraham's willingness to share his land with Lot, children can practice sharing materials with one another. The next week the same story, told a different way, can lead to activities that help them learn to let another person choose first, as Abraham did.

We can use the early childhood period of unquestioning belief to assure children of God's love and personal care, to lay a foundation of trust and confidence in His Word, and to foster positive attitudes toward fellowship and prayer that will continue to enrich their worship. If we teach so that children's biblical understanding can be expanded as they grow, rather than having to be corrected, our children as adolescents may not have to go through the storms of doubt and confusion in which so many founder. Learning Christ's love and forgiveness from their earliest years, they will truly go from faith to faith.

The Elementary School Years, Age 6 to 11

The child enters this period a dependent, impressionable novice, at the mercy of his own perceptions, circumscribed by the small world of himself, his family, and a few friends, and limited by his still undeveloped powers of thought. He leaves it five years later a knowledgeable, literate (in a minimal sense), and self-contained pre-adult, reasonably aware of the history and science of his culture, and intellectually capable of evaluating himself and his experiences. During these later years of childhood his personality and beliefs have been consolidated. He is ready to test the waters of adolescence. Whether he sinks or swims will depend in part on how the supervising adults in his life have prepared him to make hard decisions.

How the School-age Child Thinks

It is possible to trace in the school-age child the same patterns of thought that characterized him as a preschooler. The patterns, however, are undergoing transformation —great changes have already taken place. *Egocentric thinking persists, but is rooted firmly in reality.* The mentally healthy school-age child can distinguish his feelings and experiences from other people's, although his are decidedly more important. He grasps the meaning of ownership and realizes that using something does not mean it belongs to him. He can understand and sympathize with another's pain.

The relationships of cause and effect are clearer. He can "back up" or reverse his reasoning, and look for other than immediate causes behind events. *Able now to consider several elements of a situation at once,* the child is better at seeing the larger picture. In fact, he is often fascinated by complexity and detail, and he enriches his understanding by observation. However, he is still not a possibility thinker; he considers what is, not what might be.

A notable gain over early childhood is *the ability to think logically about concrete experiences.* During this period, Mary Wilcox says, "Children discover how to organize and classify those objects and actions which can be seen, heard, tasted, felt, or otherwise experienced in concrete ways."[10] They are not comfortable with hypothetical ideas or intangible realities; a much heard expression in the classroom is, "I don't *get* it!" Although this age child has learned to correct his perceptions logically, he is not yet able to deal with things beyond his perception. Like our friends from Missouri, he has got to be shown.

Because impressive amounts of learning take place during school years, adults sometimes assume understanding where it does not exist. Children this age continue the tendency to *distort new information to fit into their own mental structure.* Thinking is so literal that many abstract theological concepts are misunderstood. Asked by a researcher how Jesus replied to Satan's suggestion that He turn stones into bread, one child answered correctly, "He said man does not live by bread alone." Asked what Jesus meant by that, she said, "I guess He meant they should put butter or jam on it." While the child may be able to verbalize the meaning of baptism and explain the elements of communion, he often fails to grasp the deeper significance of identifying with Christ in His suffering, death, and Resurrection. The child is still a believer, but his beliefs are as yet pre-theological.

Learning and Development During the School Years

An awesome range of abilities and characteristics are

spanned in the elementary years. In an attempt to narrow the area under discussion, we will consider children in age groups of two years.

Primaries, Age 6 and 7, Grades 1 and 2

At age six a child's life changes drastically. Having completed kindergarten and perhaps nursery school, he is faced for the first time with the serious academic tasks of childhood: learning to read, write, compute, and cope with the pressures of school life. Gone forever is the comfortable pace of early childhood, lived in the refuge of home, Mommy, and long afternoon naps.

Happily, most six-year-olds are ready for the change. They welcome opportunities to learn and look forward, however temporarily, to the grown-up responsibilities of lunch boxes and homework. At the same time church teachers should be aware that for many children first grade means a certain amount of trauma. Coupled with a full day of school are the conflicts that invariably arise with large numbers of children on school buses and playgrounds and in crowded lunchrooms. In most schools, the six-year-old is low man on a very insensitive totem pole of older schoolmates.

Church programs for six- and seven-year-olds should be a haven of personal attention, pleasant surroundings, and freedom from anxiety. Primary church leaders will find it to their advantage and the children's benefit to keep student-teacher ratios low, and groups of children below twenty. By third or fourth grade children will be adjusted to school routines. They will have mastered essential study skills and be ready to work more independently.

Primary children are a delight to teach. Eager and responsive, affectionate and inquisitive, they are still open to adult influence and are anxious to please. In their optimism they sometimes overestimate themselves and their abilities. It is especially true of this age that "the spirit is willing, but the flesh is weak." Primaries tire easily; they are prone to illnesses. Attendance and attentiveness both fluctuate in primary classrooms—times for rest, relaxation, and review must be built into the program.

Intellectually the six- to seven-year-old is reaching for a new level of reasoning ability. His thought processes have speeded up. By the end of second grade most children will be securely in the stage of cognitive development that Piaget calls *concrete operations:* the child now reasons logically about things he has had direct, concrete experiences with. He can do in his head what he formerly had to do with his hands. He does not have to count blocks to add 2 plus 3; he can picture it in his head. When recalling the story of Jonah, instead of *acting it out,* he is able to *think it through.*

Still several years in the future is the ability to reason about abstract ideas—things he cannot form a picture of— but beginning now and until about age eleven, the child absorbs a massive amount of information. It will fuel the furnace of his thought as an abstract-reasoning adolescent.

The Middle Elementary Years, Age 8 and 9, Grades 3 and 4

Eight- and nine-year-olds, sometimes called middlers, are stronger and better coordinated than they were as primaries. They can work for longer periods without tiring. They are eager to test their skills in projects and even research assignments, if the work is made to sound interesting. Important at this age is the child's drive to achieve competency. Middlers are struggling for the assurance that they can cope with life's demands—that they can accomplish and achieve.

Just as early childhood experiences in acting upon information developed the school-age ability to reason about it, so during the school years the accumulation of facts and experiences is foundational to later understanding. For this reason the middle school years should be increasingly rich in Bible content. Fact can now be built on fact and can be seen in relation to other facts. Because the child is able to consider several related facts at the same time, generalizations can be formed, principles can be derived. By age nine a sense of time and space is beginning to emerge so that chronology and map study have meaning. Better able now to *decenter* his thinking, the middler child can understand another's point of view. He becomes interested in different cultures and other forms of life. He can listen and respond intelligently to another person's ideas. Formerly it was difficult even to take turns talking; now he can converse. Moreover, children this age *need* to exchange ideas and opinions. They need to talk to one another and to their teachers. As they mature they should be given opportunities to share experiences in small groups, to discuss and debate. They should be able to reflect aloud the meaning of Scripture in their lives.

Spiritual Needs of Primaries and Middlers

The concrete-operational child is developing a true conscience; he begins to understand that certain acts are intrinsically wrong, whether or not anyone finds out and punishes him. He often feels guilty. He needs to be led to find forgiveness in Christ, and the assurance of His support and help in overcoming temptation.

The primary child has many fears; he needs to know that God is a "very present help in trouble," and to experience brave David's testimony, "What time I am afraid I will trust in thee." The older child of eight or nine is often ashamed of his fears and launches an all-out attack on them by watching horror shows and talking tough. Some are not above shoving their fears off on a younger child. They need to learn compassion and responsibility for the weaker brother—an advanced step in the decentering process that will not be fully achieved until maturity, but we can help them begin. Nine-year-olds are preoccupied with justice. Wilcox says children this age are "filled with an urgency to make things come out even."[11] We must present him with biblical episodes of moral dilemmas and choices: David and Saul, Ruth and Naomi, the Samaritan and the injured Jew. The middler, too, must learn to make moral choices.

The Junior Years—Age 10 and 11, Grades 5 and 6

These are the years that Arnold Gesell calls "the foothills of adolescence," when the child's thoughts and behavior remind us that he has started the long ascent toward adulthood. Subtle but significant differences in his approach to life need to be reflected in changes in what the church programs for him. The junior boy or girl is a social creature, still close to the family but forming deeper and lasting friendships among peers. Juniors' social interests play no small part in keeping them involved in church programs, particularly the "optional" ones like children's church.

Physically the ten-to-eleven-year-old is in peak condition. His motor control is excellent, and childhood diseases are mostly behind him. He loves to dig into a project and will spend inordinate amounts of time getting the details perfect. Get this age involved in making a model of Solomon's temple, and they will create a splendor to rival the original. Toward the end of age eleven a spurt of preadolescent growth may cause frequent fatigue. Emotional and physical fluctuations occur, particularly among girls, who are likely to precede boys in maturation. Nevertheless, the junior has his emotional, physical, and intellectual abilities well in hand. This is a prime period for spiritual decision and growth.

Though still a concrete thinker, the junior has a thirst for facts and information which will serve him well in building Bible knowledge if the proper resources are made available to him. He learns well on his own. He is now adept at reversing his thinking to check his conclusions—something he could not quite pull off a few years ago. He is able to distinguish the trivial from the essential, to relate similar elements, and to classify with increasing skill. Verbal ability is catching up with hand dexterity; he has been able for some time to create clever puppets and stage effects, now he can write a decent plot to go with them.

A major task of Christian education during this period is to bridge the cultural gap between Bible times and ours. The youngster must have repeated and varied experiences in applying Scripture to the circumstances of life. Formerly he could not see the many possibilities inherent in a situation, and he was not good at foreseeing consequences. Now, on the brink of adolescence, he struggles toward the highest level of mental ability which Piaget calls *formal (or abstract) operations*. These greater mental powers will allow him to consider hypothetical ideas and to gain insight into biblical metaphors and similies once too obscure for him. Many juniors are conscious of a need to think more deeply than they once did; worship and learning activities for juniors must be strengthened to satisfy this need.

Spiritual Development of Juniors

The junior looks to heroes of history and Scripture for models of what he himself would like to be. He is contemplating the future and forming opinions about what might be desirable careers. Lifetime directions are being established. Children who have not professed Christ should be given every opportunity to do so. Juniors should have exposure to Bible heroes, to giants of church history, to missionaries and other Christians in ministry they can admire and emulate. The men and women who lead them (and juniors especially need teachers of both sexes) should provide ideal role models of Christian character and attractiveness.

Adult leaders must be sensitive to the fact that many youngsters begin in sixth grade the fundamental reassessment of values so well-known of junior highs. During this pivotal time preadolescents often experience confusion as they try to fit former, concrete ideas about God and His working into a more mature theological framework. We can assist the junior's theological ideas to mature with him by helping him wrestle personally with the moral and spiritual issues the Bible presents. With the Spirit's guidance, many juniors are ready to interpret the Bible meaningfully. The junior who is sure of his faith in Christ can become an active participant in witness and worship. This will require a different kind of church-time program from those planned for younger children. Gradually, the junior should be led to the place where he feels increasingly a part of the adult congregation.

All Children Learn According to Their Way

In this chapter we have considered the special ways a child learns as he develops. However, there is much about human learning we have not discussed. Many other factors affect learning besides development: the physical environment affects it, rewards and punishment affect it, the individual's self-concept and the teacher's attitude and training affect it. We have said almost nothing about these things, although they are important. Our purpose here has been to describe the stages of a child's development, particularly his intellectual development, which cause him to perceive things differently at one age than at another. As we consider the spectrum of development and abilities across the years of childhood, we can generalize a few important learning principles.

1. *Children of all ages learn from concrete experiences.* Young children learn by acting on information and manipulating objects—toys, models, puzzles, play equipment. Older children learn from actual or simulated events, from stories and lessons that provide direct experiences through role play, dramatization, field trips, and projects. At every age concrete experiences must precede verbal experiences.

2. *Given a good base of concrete experiences, children can learn a great deal from verbal and written materials.* The levels of learning are not fixed compartments sealed off from one another. Sometimes learners retreat to an earlier, more concrete stage; sometimes they leap ahead to more advanced thinking. It is unlikely that the preschool child is completely intuitive in his approach or that the preadolescent is completely verbal, but at a given stage of development one mode of learning predominates. Knowing our age group helps us choose suitable Bible content, methods, and materials for successful learning.

3. *At any age, a child learns best from his own activity.* Children must act on things to understand them. When the teacher tries to bypass this need, the result is superficial learning. The Christian teacher's task therefore, is threefold: to structure a

curriculum the child can comprehend, to provide a wide variety of interesting materials the child can use, and to present challenging spiritual truths on which he may act.

This is how the child learns. Proverbs 22:6 has told it straight. If the child is to learn God's truth for all time, for today as well as tomorrow, for youth and old age and eternity, we must nourish him early and well. Knowing his patterns of growth, we must suit methods and content to his stage of development. We must teach him according to his way.

Notes

1. F. Delitzsche, *Proverbs*, vol. 6, *Old Testament Commentaries* (Grand Rapids: Wm. B. Eerdmans Publishing Co., 1975), pp. 86-87.
2. *The New Berkely Version in Modern English*, rev. ed. (Grand Rapids: Zondervan Publishing House, 1969).
3. *The Jerusalem Bible* (Garden City: Doubleday, 1966).
4. R. F. Horton, *The Expositor's Bible* (New York: Hodder and Stoughton, n.d.).
5. Matthew Henry, *Proverbs*, vol. 3, *Commentary* (New York: Revell, n.d.).
6. As quoted in Lawrence O. Richards, *A Theology of Christian Education* (Grand Rapids: Zondervan Publishing House, 1975), p. 187.
7. Leslie A. Hart, *How the Brain Works* (n.p.: Basic Books, 1975), p. 187.
8. Ross Campbell, M.D., *How to Really Love Your Child* (Wheaton: Victor Books/Scripture Press, 1977), p. 44.
9. Ibid., p. 42.
10. Mary M. Wilcox, *Developmental Journey* (Nashville: Abingdon Press, 1979).
11. Ibid., p. 55.

3

Questions You May Have about Children's Church

Now a certain church went forth to the highways and hedges, and lo, they beheld a great multitude. "There are much families in this place," they said. "We must compel them to come in. We must plan elective Bible study courses, and fine music and preaching in the sanctuary, and a coffee hour for fellowship. In this way they will hear the Word and believe."

"But what of their little ones?" asked another. "Will not their children prevent them? Will they not weigh heavily upon their parents, and disrupt the sounds of worship, and knock over the coffee cups? What shall be done with them?"

"We will find caretakers for the children," said another, "so they may be watched and hinder not their parents." So caretakers were found to keep watch over the children, each in his own turn, Sunday by Sunday. And the parents worshiped and rejoiced in God, and the children ran and played.

What Is the Purpose of Children's Church?

Before a church makes any plans for children during the worship hour, leaders must ask penetrating questions. Why do we want this program? What is our purpose? What do we seek to accomplish? Have we the simple, pragmatic goal of providing for the children while the grown-ups worship? Is our purpose to extend the teaching time so more Bible learning can take place? Or do we want our program to inspire children themselves to worship?

A clear purpose makes decisions much easier. Purpose provides direction for grouping, location, staffing, and choosing material. One congregation has an evangelistic purpose for their children's church.[1] Their bus ministry brings in large numbers of unchurched children every week. As children disgorge from the buses they are funneled into large assembly rooms where the gospel is presented each Sunday and children are invited to accept Christ. The Sunday school hour follows worship and concentrates on Bible learning and its application to the Christian life.

Another church feels that the purpose of their program is to prepare children for worship with the larger congregation. To this end, children are ushered quietly into a room with pews, hymnbooks, and a reverent atmosphere. A printed children's bulletin leads them through an order of service much like the one taking place in the sanctuary.

A third church feels that the child's worship experience should allow for much expression, creative activity, and involvement, with little of the formalities associated with adult worship. Their program emphasizes small groups.

Approaches to children's church vary, just as the style of worship may differ from one congregation to another. What matters is that the program (1) be consistent with the church's overall goals in Christian education, and (2) focus on worship, leading the child to admire God's Person and praise His works. Everything in the immediate environment, that is, every act of the teachers and every song, story, and creative project (should there be any), every bulletin board, and visual aid, must serve the ultimate purpose of worship. Although the program may be more active and physical than would an adult service, the objective is the same—to help individuals adore God and love each other.

When children enter, they should become conscious of a special atmosphere: the room is a virtual laboratory for Christian living where members practice "building others up...Being kind and compassionate to one another, forgiving each other," as Ephesians 4:29, 32 (NIV) admonish, and where Jesus is the focus of praise and the subject of song. Informal activities like snacks and games promote fellowship and conversation—positive interactions among children and teachers.

In everything the early church provides the model for children as well as for adults in the church: Luke tells us "the whole group of believers was united, heart and soul," (Acts 4:32) and, "they shared food gladly and generously; they praised God..." (Acts 2:47, JB).

Have you specified what your purposes are for your particular children's church program? Do you know *why* the program deserves the time and effort it will entail? If so, you can get down to the practical questions of Where? When? and Who? (Later chapters will consider What? and How?)

Where and When Should Children's Worship be Conducted?

These are just about the easiest decisions you will make! As you balance your purposes against your facilities and church schedule, the best time and location will soon emerge.

Time: In most cases children's worship is held simultaneously with the adult service. Let us assume that your church follows the familiar Sunday-school-first-hour, worship-second-hour pattern, with a fifteen minute break in between. Let us also assume that your aim is to provide a worship experience for children at various age levels.

Ideally, worship should follow instruction; the child's heart has already been prepared to consider God and His acts. He has been enriched and stimulated during the Sunday school hour. Worship should be a culmination of the learning activities of the morning and should follow immediately upon the teaching hour.

The church that we attend provides a thirty-minute fellowship hour between Sunday school and the morning service. When we began our children's church program several years ago, we decided to share that half-hour with Sunday school. The teaching program now ends at 10:45, and children's church starts then. We learned quickly that a smooth transition *matters.* For this reason children's church workers are always on hand before Sunday school ends—if not in the room (which may disturb some programs), then waiting just outside the door. A few children leave after Sunday school, some show up just in time for worship, but most children remain through the transition, busy and occupied and scarcely conscious of a changing of the guard.

Location: When the children's church movement first became popular, proponents advised churches to provide a special "chapel" for the program. The "miniature church" setting at first had great appeal. However, workers soon found that this formal structure limited children's worship activities to sitting, standing, singing, and listening. There is not much else you can do in a pew! If children are going to respond to God with their entire beings, the facilities must be flexible enough to let them do it.

The best location for your children's church program is probably in the same rooms where Sunday school is held. These are usually well located near fire exits, bathrooms, and the library or media center. The Sunday school room furniture is the proper size for the age and classroom materials can be shared by both groups. Especially with younger groups, the less traveling around that has to be done, the better. Using the same room all morning also establishes a sense of continuity.

If another room must be used, choose it with care. Remember that a large room with undefined space (like a fellowship hall) invites more physical activity—running, jumping, falling! Better to use a few adjoining rooms or one large one with moveable partitions. Flexibility is the key word. A children's worship program often entails a variety of activities. One cluster of children may need to work on a mural while another group plans a skit or rehearses a choir number. Still another area should be set apart for worship. If your group is small, one room will suffice; simply arrange the classroom furniture into well-defined activity centers. Further information on rooms and facilities will be discussed in later chapters.

Diagram A
Possible Locations for Children's Church

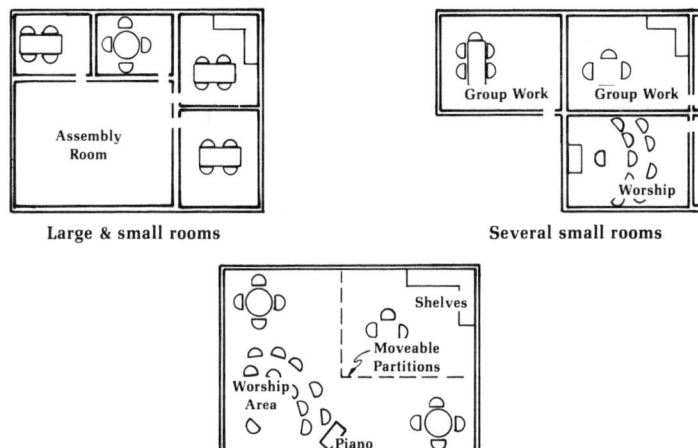

What Age-levels Should Worship Together?

Whenever possible, children's church should follow the same age-group divisions that are used in the Sunday school. The same titles can also be used: beginner church (or if you prefer, beginners worship), primary church, junior church, and so on. If attendance is lower during the second hour, some grades may be combined.

Ideally, three-year-olds should have a room to themselves, while fours and fives, who are more mature socially, can worship together. Children of elementary school age work very well in two-year groupings—first and second grades, third and fourth, fifth and sixth. While noticeable differences in skills and reasoning do exist, they seldom hinder communication.

Fewer problems arise when children of the same age can learn and worship together; however, churches should not feel that because they cannot offer ideal groupings they should forget children's worship altogether. Far from it! Most children will participate better in their own service, even if it is not ideally structured, than they would with adults in the sanctuary.

In addition, benefits can accrue from the experiences of a mixed age group, if teachers know how to take advantage of them. Older children can help younger ones; the more mature children can be models for the immature ones. A large group can stimulate feelings of unity and strength in corporate worship. The one basic requirement for grouping is to separate preschoolers (kindergarten and younger) from older children who have reading, writing, and reasoning skills. If only one children's church service can be offered, by all means start with preschoolers (they need it most) and add a separate program for school-age children as soon as possible. Then, as attendance reaches twenty or thirty, the groups can be divided again. The chart below suggests possible arrangements.

Minimum divisions   Divisions as groups enlarge

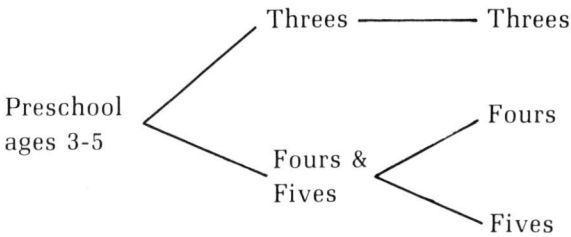

Groups should subdivide again if they grow larger than 20 in attendance.

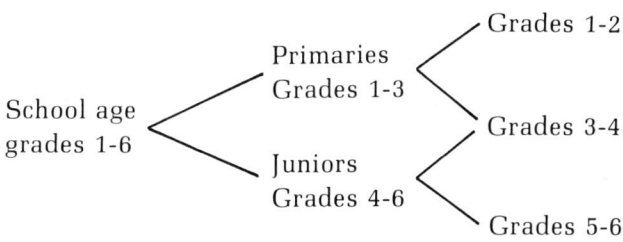

Groups should subdivide again if they grow larger than 30 in attendance.

Do Children of Ten and Eleven Really Need a Child's Worship Service?

Christian educators often disagree on this point. Many feel that age-level worship should be provided for all children. Others respond that tens and elevens can sit reasonably well through an adult service and profit from it. Again, each church must examine its own purposes. Have you large numbers of children from unchurched homes who would be at loose ends (or, worse yet, not present at all) in the adult service? If so, you may especially need the training in worship that a junior church program provides.

If, on the other hand, it is important to you that older children learn to participate in congregational worship, you may prefer that fifth and sixth graders attend church with their parents. Eleven-year-olds are beginning to think abstractly—a giant step in development that allows them to understand some concepts in hymns and sermons that once confused them. A later chapter will explore in greater detail ways that churches can adapt their programs to the special needs of fifth and sixth graders.

What about Staff and Responsibilities?

The most important factor in the success of your children's church program is the people who lead it. Choose them carefully. They should be individuals who love children and have a background of successful ministry with them. They should have high expectations concerning the value of the program and of the capability of children for genuine worship of God. Repeated studies have made clear the positive correlation between teachers' expectations and the level at which students achieve. Those who expect good performance and behavior are more likely to get it.

The children's church staff should represent both men and women. Older teens who are capable and effective with children can be trained to be valuable team members. When they are used, they should be considered full staff workers, attending all meetings and accepting full teaching responsibilities. Supervising adults would have a special obligation to develop the talents and increase the skills of a teen teacher.

How Many Workers Will Be Needed?

The number of staff members needed will depend upon the size of your group and the nature of your program. An hour-long formal service where most of the action is teacher-led requires fewer workers than does a more varied, child-centered program. Aim to secure enough teachers so that no one is overworked. That will keep teachers happier and reduce the amount of turnover among workers. A student-teacher ratio of 1 to 4 in preschool and 1 to 8 for older groups will help teachers meet children's individual needs.

How Can We Avoid Recruitment Problems?

Churches that have difficulty staffing children's church usually report the same response from potential workers: "I don't want to miss the worship service every Sunday." And their concern is justified—adults need worship, too! There is no easy way to get around this problem, but here is how some churches handle it.

1. *Give each children's church worker a tape of the morning worship service.* One large church in our area has done this successfully for years. Workers return their tapes each Sunday morning and receive them back after the service. While a tape is

not as good as being there, it lasts longer and can be replayed many times!

2. *Emphasize the Sunday evening service.* Workers do have opportunity to worship with the congregation if they attend the evening service regularly. All Christians need to share in the ordinance of Communion. Hold it on Sunday evening so nursery workers and children's church staff can participate.

3. *Give staff a summer break.* Consider the benefits of closing down children's worship programs during July and August, except for the youngest departments. Children have a chance to sit with their parents and practice what they learned about participating in the worship service. (If they find the sermon somewhat long and wearying they will doubly appreciate children's church when it opens in the fall!) In addition, staff members welcome the opportunity to worship with the rest of the congregation for two months. There is little doubt that the prospect of a summer break makes serving full time in children's church more attractive to volunteers.

4. *Have two worship services on Sunday morning.* Large churches do this for reasons of space, or to relieve parking problems. Could not double worship services be held to meet the needs of staff? Naturally, a small church struggling to fill the sanctuary *once* in the morning will not want to try doing it twice! But consider the possibility of holding the first service in a Sunday school room. Important features like the choir and organ will be missing, of course, but hymns, prayers, and the message would be identical. Your pastor may find that he *likes* practicing his sermon on a small group

first!
5. Churches that choose curriculum with the goal of unifying the entire Sunday morning program for children have still another option: *having Sunday school and children's church staff alternate time slots every quarter.*

   Before you reject this idea as impractical, ask, Why not? Would not it be more equitable than asking the same workers to miss church services all year? Would not all workers benefit from getting to know each others' goals and problems? The program can be set up in one of two ways. Either the staffs switch programs, teaching Sunday school one quarter and children's church the next, or the programs switch, with children's worship held *first* during alternating quarters. The change for children is minimal—they see the same adults, but at different times during the morning. In a few cases, children who normally come to only one program find out they are missing something!

What *Not* to Do!

Some churches have attempted to solve staffing problems by having two leadership teams in children's church, each serving a two- or three-week shift. It is not hard to imagine the confusion this causes. Steady progress is almost impossible and the change in personnel is hard on children, who need close, long-term relationships with the adults who would teach them. In a one-hour-a-week situation, it is hard enough to establish relationships, without the whole thing changing every few weeks.

Accentuate the Positive

When recruiting staff do not apologize for asking workers to miss worship if they must in order to work in children's church. Remember that leaders are worshiping even as they serve. The psalmist knew that our service could be an offering of praise to God: "Praise the Lord, you who serve Him, Serving in the house of the Lord, in the courts of the house of our God! Praise the Lord, for the Lord is good" (Ps. 135:1-3, JB). Perhaps this is especially true of worship with children. More than once I have felt sorry for the staid and silent adults in the sanctuary who could not join in the heartfelt prayers and hopeful songs sent Godward from Primary Church II.

What are the Specific Responsibilities of Staff Members?

Many churches appoint a coordinator who has general responsibility for all children's worship programs. The lead teacher in each unit reports to the coordinator, who may be the Christian education director, the preschool or children's division coordinator, the chairperson of the Christian education committee, or some other responsible person. Since each level of children's church functions as a separate unit, the coordinator's job is to assist leaders in maintaining a successful and smoothly functioning program. He or she helps to recruit staff, serves as a resource person, and, perhaps most importantly, acts as communications link between children's church and related agencies. In some cases the coordinator also evaluates the program and seeks resources, facilities, and training opportunities to strengthen it.

**Diagram B
Organizational**

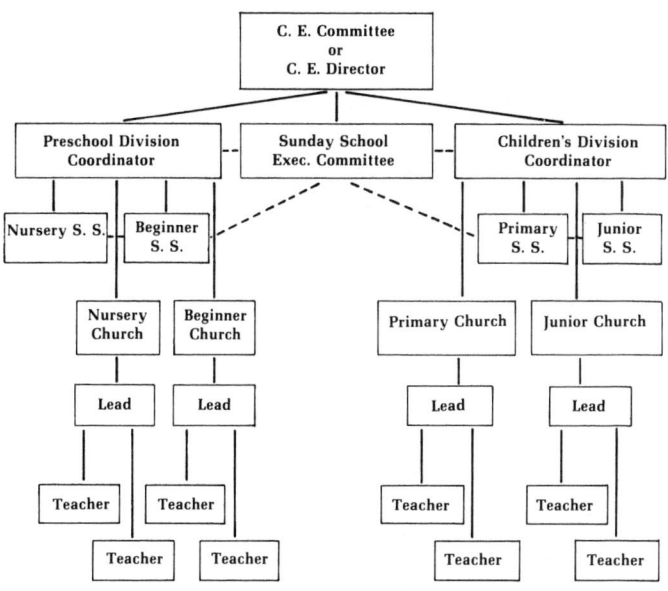

Responsibilities of the Lead Teacher

The lead teacher of each children's church department is a key person. In addition to her or his qualifications for children's ministry the lead teacher must be able to inspire and work with other teachers. Job descriptions adapted to your church's needs and distributed to all workers will help them do a better job. Generally, the lead teacher's duties would include the following:

1. Leads the worship service each week, or arranges for another teacher to do it.
2. Leads monthly meetings with teachers to study the curriculum, plan services, and assign responsibilities.
3. Works closely with the Sunday school department superintendent so that the two agencies mesh and reinforce each other.
4. Prepares the room weekly so that supplies are in hand, bulletin boards are attractive, and the room is clean, colorful, and conducive to worship.
5. Studies each child personally to know his background, interests, parents, and other programs he attends at church. Discerns individual needs and seeks to meet them through the church-time program.
6. Arranges for smooth transitions. Arrives in the room early and leaves only after every child has gone and the room is in order.
7. Contacts a qualified substitute whenever a teacher will be absent.
8. Provides extra activities for those Sundays when church extends past the usual hour.
9. Maintains contact with parents through informative letters and meetings. When appropriate, contacts parents personally concerning their child's special contribution to the group, or his particular need.
10. Reports at regular intervals to the coordinator or whoever administers the program. Informs him or pastor of children who make a profession of faith.

11. Cooperates with other agency leaders to share names and addresses of new children.
12. Arranges for special features in the program—missionary speakers, visits from the pastor or Christian education director, etc.

Responsibilities of the Teacher

1. Prepares to lead a small group or special feature of the program each week. Participates fully in all other activities.
2. Is prepared to assume leadership of the worship program in the absence of or at the request of the lead teacher.
3. Attends monthly planning meetings and any other planned activity. Contributes ideas and talents.
4. Gets to know each child on a personal basis.
5. Is on hand before Sunday school ends to help set up materials and remains after the program until the room is in order.
6. Shares in the preparation of snacks, visual aids, bulletin boards, and other materials needed in the program.

In addition to those requirements listed above which may apply, teachers should be informed concerning the amount of time each week that will be required for preparation. All workers should understand the importance of making individual children and the program as a whole a subject of continuous prayer.

How Is Children's Church Related to Other Agencies of the Church?

As churches expand their ministries to children, the task of correlating programs becomes increasingly important. Many churches are finding that a good way to do this is to appoint a division coordinator for ministries in each age group. The preschool coordinator covers agencies for those ages two through five. The children's division coordinator works with leaders from all agencies who serve the six to eleven age group—for example, Sunday school department superintendents, Pioneer Girls and Brigade leaders, children's choir directors and, of course, children's church workers. The coordinator's task is not to direct all these programs, but to harmonize them. Because he or she knows the programs well, he is able to funnel information from one group to another and can serve as a resource person to all.

Children's Church and Sunday School

We mentioned earlier in the chapter the importance of leaders in both these agencies working closely together. If no coordinator is available, it is doubly important that leaders keep in constant touch. In every way possible, the programs of Sunday school and children's church should work together to serve children's spiritual needs. The Sunday school's function is instructional; the church hour's inspirational. Curriculum and activities should complement each other, never conflict or overlap. If the department superintendent and the children's church lead teacher understand each other's curriculum and purposes, if they talk over goals and problems regularly, they will build their ministries into what, ideally, they should provide for children: a unified Sunday morning experience of Bible learning and Christian worship.

Other Agencies

Since children's church activities seldom reach beyond the worship hour, there is less danger of conflict with weekday programs. However, the left hand should always know what the right hand is doing, if only to prevent the children's hearing about Gideon's victory over the Midianites three times in one week. Also, leaders of all agencies should be apprised of scheduled events and special programs. Good communication with children's club and choir leaders will help church-time teachers support and promote these activities. Again, the division coordinator can be the organizational link joining all these agencies.

What about Evangelism in Children's Church?

Nothing is more important than an individual's relationship with God. This is as true of children as it is of adults. At every level, we want to be sure that our lessons and activities direct the child to faith in Jesus Christ. Evangelism will take different forms with each age level.

With *preschoolers* a preevangelism emphasis should build trust in God, preparing the child for the day when a true understanding of salvation and the Spirit's conviction of personal need will prompt him to receive Christ.

Primaries sometimes express a desire to receive Christ as Savior. Those who do should be counselled individually in language they can comprehend. Primaries can understand that God wants to forgive their sins, accept their faith, and make them His children, members of His family. They should not be confused by being told that

"Jesus changes our black hearts and makes them pure and white." Primaries take these analogies literally and miss their true meaning. It is never necessary to pressure primaries to believe; teachers should simply be available and sensitive when a child indicates an awareness of his need.

Junior children, especially at ten and eleven, are at a better age to make spiritual decisions. When the gospel is presented meaningfully, without undue pressure, many can respond sincerely to an invitation to receive Christ. The children's church hour is an ideal time to do this. Check your junior curriculum material. Are evangelistic opportunities offered winsomely and at appropriate intervals? If not, you may want to supplement with other materials. For helpful information on evangelism of children, see Zuck and Clark, *Childhood Education in the Church*, pp. 153-166, or the ICL concept booklet, *Outreach to Children*, Regal Books, Glendale, CA.

Can Special Children Be Provided for in Children's Church?

Most churches that really want to, find that they can provide the same services for retarded children that they do for others; however, additional space and personnel are usually required. Excellent materials are available to help willing church teachers—many are listed in Chapter 8. While special training for teachers is valuable, it is not essential.

If your church has a special education director, he or she is the best person to recruit staff and help develop the program. Parents of retarded youngsters are often knowledgeable about services and opportunities for the retarded. Enlist their help in finding people to assist in your program.

In some instances a physically or mentally handicapped child can be included in the regular children's church program. They may require the full-time attention of a volunteer to help them participate. This is a small price to pay for the enriching opportunities their presence offers to the other students and to the program as a whole.

Gloria Hawley, in her inspiring little book, *How to Teach the Mentally Retarded,* offers practical advice to churches who want to reach out to the handicapped:

> Retarded individuals, and their families, are within most communities. Look into the special schools in your vicinity. Attend the PTA sessions there and talk to the parents. Go to your city hall and ask about the programs for the retarded. Observe a few sessions of any programs in your community for the retarded and get to know the parents. Go to any activities in your area for the retarded, such as the Special Olympics. Write to the National Association for Retarded Citizens in your area. Special people are in the sphere of your influence![2]

If your church is blessed with one or more of these special "little ones," remember that you are as responsibile for him as for any other child. God has put him in your sphere of influence. He will help you find those with the gifts and abilities to help the special child.

In this chapter we have discussed basic questions about the nature and scope of your program. Whatever that program is, it should have on it the stamp of your originality. There is no church exactly like yours, so you should not expect to reproduce anyone else's program. Study your situation to design the kind of children's worship program your church needs and can maintain. Then get on with making it work.

Notes

1. Charles F. Schiede, Sr. "But We Never Did it That Way Before!" *Evangelizing Today's Child.* vol. 6, no. 6 (1979), pp. 14-17.
2. Gloria H. Hawley, *How to Teach the Mentally Retarded* (Wheaton: Victor Books/Scripture Press, 1979), p. 15.

4

Providing an Environment for Worship

"Worship is the highest outcome in Christian education. . . .Worship is at the heart of what the church is and does. 'The single unique function of the church is the worshiping of God. This is one activity no other group attempts.'"[1]

"The first and foremost response of the persons involved in the church is worship."[2]

Do you agree with the strong statements on worship quoted above? Do they express your understanding of the nature and function of the church? Some may contend that the first response of persons involved in the church should be *repentance*, followed by worship. But I wonder if worship does not more often lead to repentance than the other way around. Isaiah saw the Lord high and lifted up and knew that he was "undone. . .a man of unclean lips" (Isa. 6:5). Saul the Pharisee, overwhelmed by a heavenly light and Voice, "trembling and astonished said, Lord, what wilt thou have me to do?" (Acts 9:6). When God is lifted up in His holiness, power, and compassion, hearts touched by His Spirit respond in worship and repentance.

The act of worshiping God distinguishes the gathered church from any other human assembly. While people everywhere seek to satisfy their innate yearning to adore one greater than themselves, many do so falsely, worshiping "they know not what." It is uniquely the believing congregation that worships God "in spirit and in truth." Since we have Jesus' testimony that the Father prizes such worship (John 4:23), we ought to be concerned that the individuals in our care experience it as God intended.

The fact is that surprisingly little attention has been given to worship in Christian education programs for children. In the past, worship for the young has been limited to Sunday school "opening exercises" and whatever the child could fathom of the adult service. Unfortunately, opening exercises were seldom more than a means of "getting everyone off to a good start" with some rousing choruses, or worse, giving late comers a chance to slip in unobtrusively. With good reason, many Sunday schools have dropped the opening session in favor of more productive class-time activities. Adult leaders should be aware, however, that the lack of genuine worship improverishes the child. Paul Vieth reminds us, "To worship God is a basic human need, as real as the need for food and human companionship and other values that give life meaning. This is as true for the young child as for the mature man or woman."[3]

It is also true that children as well as adults may worship falsely. The ancients believed that worship of the Lord God must be taught. The writer of Psalm 78 vowed not to conceal instruction in worship from children, but to "tell to the generation to come the praises of the Lord, and His strength and His wondrous works that He has done" (Ps. 78:4, NASB).

Today, for the first time in modern church life, and thanks largely to the growth of interest in children's church, the young are being offered worship opportunities they can participate in rather than merely observe. The second hour program is (or should be) designed especially to lead children to worship God. This leaves the Sunday school teacher free to use the entire first hour for Bible learning activities. Excellent materials and a variety of curriculums are available for churches to use in children's worship programs. Careful correlation of worship with Sunday school lessons can make Sunday morning a total ministry of Bible learning and worship for children. Robert Johnson, a Sunday school leader for three decades, challenged his denomination (Baptist General Conference) in 1979: "Learning and worship should not be separated. We need to think of the two hours together on Sunday mornings—Sunday school *and* worship."

Choosing Materials for the Worship Hour

Prayerful consideration should be given to the material to be used in children's church. To a great extent, the curriculum will set the direction and determine the activities in the program. If workers are left to select haphazardly any materials that appeal to them, the final results will be chaotic. Instead, a committee of teachers and church leaders appointed by the Christian education committee should be responsible to select material. After studying carefully the church's objectives for worship of both adults and children (see Chapter 3) the committee should seek materials that will help implement those objectives. Fortunately, more and better quality resources for worship are being published each year. We will discuss those most likely to be suited to Alliance churches. Other good materials are listed in the Appendix section.

Why Can We Not Develop Our Own Curriculum?

Only a few churches brave the hazards of developing their own worship programs, and most of those efforts fail after a short while. Curriculum writing is a time-consuming and demanding task; rarely does a church have the resources to accomplish it. In most cases published materials, adapted to meet local needs, provide a sound and balanced curriculum.

Criteria for Choosing Curriculum

In choosing any materials, the church's first concerns should always be (1) *Is the material biblically sound?* and (2) *Will it fulfill our objectives for this program?* With priority given to these essentials, a children's church curriculum should also meet these criteria—

3. *Does the content correlate well with Sunday school curriculum?*

    Have you ever tested a group of church teens and been appalled at their garbled understanding of Bible chronology? This all-too-familiar phenomenon may result from bad curriculum planning: the student's Christian education has been a spotty affair of many different curriculums for short periods of time. The church's curriculum plan was not unified.

    Learning requires that subjects be taught in a systematic manner. The child's progress through the church's educational program should proceed without tedious repetition of some Bible themes and omission of others. To maintain a balance of Old and New Testament, evangelism and Christian living, factual content and creative expression, give careful attention to correlation of materials in all agencies, particularly Sunday school and church time.

    When investigating worship materials, give first consideration to the publisher used by the Sunday school. Do they publish a church hour program? If so, it is probably closely correlated with Sunday school themes. At the least one could expect that lessons would not conflict or overlap, as they are likely to do if materials from different publishers are used.

4. *Is worship the true focus, or is the program actually meant for another children's ministry?*

    A true worship program must be more than a Bible story and handwork, or memory verses and evangelism; it should have worship objectives. Examine the curriculum to see what makes the program different from Sunday school, clubs, or VBS. Is its major thrust to help children learn to worship? If not, it cannot honestly fit a ministry called "Children's Church."

5. *Is provision made for differences in children's developmental and ability levels?*

    We have already discussed the vast differences in children of different ages and school experiences. A good curriculum will make ample provision in ideas and activities for children at various developmental stages.

6. *Is there an appropriate evangelistic emphasis?*

    Goals of preevangelism, evangelism, and follow-up should be served, as discussed in Chapter 3.

7. *Are activities sufficiently varied and challenging?*

    Some children's church manuals on the market repeat the same format of sit-and-listen activities every week. Others are built entirely around puppets or drama. Look for a creative balance of many methods and activities.

8. *Are visual aid and other resources available and attractive?*

    Ask yourself how helpful this curriculum will be. Is a packet of visuals and other learning aids included? If not, are available resources listed in the leader's guide? What about music? Are hymns merely listed, or is a record or songbook provided? If visuals are included, are they of good quality? Visual aids that portray crude or inferior images are worse than no visuals at all.

9. *Are teacher training features built into the leader's guide or otherwise provided for?*

   Some curriculums do an excellent job of providing books, tapes, or filmstrips to train teachers. Some include how-to pages in the front and back of the manual. Others sprinkle short training segments all through the program. Teacher development greatly enhances the value and practicality of any curriculum.

Major Evangelical Publishers

The following is a brief rundown on church-time materials produced by evangelical publishers. Each of them provides good material.

Scripture Press was among the first to publish a separate curriculum for children's worship. Programs are provided on three levels—nursery, preprimary (beginner) and primary. *Nursery Learning Programs I and II* include fifty-two complete worship programs for ages two and three. A new Bible story is presented every week. Activity packets for children are available; other resources are recommended. The programs are varied and well-paced for young children. Restful activities alternate with motion songs, story time and simple handcrafts.

Wonder Programs for preprimaries age four and five, was revised in 1978-1979. (For close correlation with Scripture Press Sunday school lessons the revised edition should be ordered.) Introductory pages give teachers helpful information concerning the program. Suggestions are included for alternate ways of presenting the Bible story and for retelling the Sunday school story when some children in the group have not heard it.

Primary Adventure Programs for grades 1 through 3, may be used for worship or for other children's ministries such as Sunday evening or midweek clubs. Each session provides a full hour of activities. Directions are given for crafts and visual aids. Additional resources are listed. A revision of the program is currently in process and will be available in 1982.

Gospel Light offers two different plans for children's worship—an expanded session for preschoolers and a complete church-time package for grade school departments. Church-hour features are included in each preschool teacher's guide for Sunday school. Weekly lessons include a page and a half of church-time content and ideas. Teachers are encouraged to act out or in other ways review the Sunday school story. A life-related story told through paper bag puppets Larry and Lisa extend the learning. Free choice activities are suggested for the early part of the session.

Church Time for Children is Gospel Light's new (1978) second hour program for children in grades 1 through 6. "Living in God's Family" and "Growing in God's Family" each consist of a boxed kit with resources for a full year of programs—an album and songbook, pictures and other visuals, puppet faces, games, and craft suggestions. The program aims at a balance of learning and worship. Outstanding features are the variety of teaching methods and resources, the training materials included, and the consistently child-centered approach. Less emphasis is placed on a formal worship structure than is true of most children's church curriculums.

David C. Cook's second hour materials, *Children's Church for Nursery, Kindergarten and Primaries* provides guide books and resources for two years of worship programs. They are planned to parallel Sunday school themes. Records, songbooks, craft manuals, and visual aid packets are available. Activities are diverse and well-chosen for each age; action rhymes are included for young children, creative activities for primaries. The worship emphasis is central. Strong points are the basic simplicity of the format and the substantial Bible content. Additional activities may need to be provided for Sundays when church runs overtime.

Over the last dozen years or so, in different situations, I have used all three of these curriculums with good results. Each has its strong points and weaknesses, but all are of high quality and can be used with confidence. While they all offer the basic content of a sound children's church program, each would require adaptions or additions to work effectively in a given church.

No kit or packaged program can guarantee that learning or worship will take place. Teachers who expect that of a curriculum expect too much. What must happen is for Spirit-filled and creative leaders *who are themselves worshipers* to adapt, expand, and improve curriculum materials according to their own children's needs. Only then can inert material lead to the mind-shaping, life-changing experience that is Christian worship.

Providing the Environment for Children's Church

One year we met in a long, bright, carpeted room, with tables convenient to the storage closet for group work, and a separate, spacious area for worship. Then our group was divided, and we were banished to the basement with two small rooms and one medium-sized one. The bulletin boards were far above the children's heads (the room was designed for adults), and the floor flooded with every heavy rain (the reason the adults left, no doubt). This year we have been crowded but happy in four small rooms with moveable walls—supremely flexible!

Church facilities are seldom ideal. Room assignments change, and church teachers rejoice when they have adequate space and learn to "maximize their potential" the rest of the time! At minimum, however, we must provide for the children we teach a safe, healthy, and pleasant environment. If they are to learn well, the surroundings must be stimulating as well as comfortable. Think for a moment of the richly complex environment into which God placed human beings—soaring mountains, lush grasslands, infinitely various plant and animal life. Think of the sights, sounds, smells, and other sensations; of a pine forest or a country meadow. Compare the great outdoors with the boxlike affairs in which we teach children. No wonder they ache to get outside!

God created people—and especially children—with a thirst for beauty, texture, and sensations from their environment. Children need colorful walls and compatable furnishings. They need art materials and musical instruments and resource books. They need maps, globes, board games, learning centers, and space to try everything out. What they need, however, may not be what they get! It takes all a teacher's determination and ingenuity to outfit a room so that children's needs are met and the worship program functions at its best. Let us start with what you need; then we will discuss briefly how to improve what you may have.

Space Needs

A rule of thumb for children's departments is that

twenty-five square feet of space is needed for each child enrolled. That assures room for diverse learning activities with freedom for adults and children to move around without bumping into furniture. A good room size is twenty or twenty-five feet in width by thirty feet in length. A much larger room is not usually conducive to good interaction and is seldom required since children's departments should be divided when they grow beyond twenty for preschoolers or thirty for grades 1 through 6.

When considering space needs, remember that children's church requires one area which can be set apart for worship even if it is only part of a room. Children should not be so crowded that learning, handcraft, refreshments, and worship all must take place in the same area. Make provision for a "worship center" which can be set up ahead of time and not be disturbed.

Walls and Floors

Psychologists know that the color of a room affects the sense of well-being of the people in the room. Individuals move more rapidly through rooms painted in dark shades; they linger in lightly colored ones. Children's rooms should be painted in soft hues which provide a good background for colorful bulletin boards and brightly painted furniture. Yellow or buff paint brightens a dark room, light green or blue cools a very sunny one. Children's rooms should have a light, airy look. Surfaces should be sound absorbing when possible. For this reason white acoustical tile and good lighting fixtures are standard for ceilings of educational buildings.

Carpeting has been shown to have a beneficial effect on the learning environment. Floors covered in commercial-grade carpeting repay the initial expense many times over.

Serviceability is high and maintenance costs low. In addition to dramatically reducing the noise level, carpet provides warmth and comfort. It permits activities on the floor, thus reducing the amount of furniture needed. It is one of the best investments a church can make in its educational facility.

Before we leave the subject of walls and lighting, let us remember that in this audio-visual age extra electrical outlets and room-darkening window shades are requirements.

Teaching Surfaces

All children's rooms should have bulletin boards mounted on the walls. A good size is three feet by six feet or up to three and one half feet by twelve feet. Boards should be mounted low, at children's eye level. Grade school rooms need ample chalkboard space as well. One blank wall, painted white or any light shade, will eliminate the need for viewing screens.

Some churches mount their bulletin boards on heavy duty hooks so they can be removed and turned around. The Sunday school then uses one side; the children's church, the other.

Furniture

Furniture for children's rooms should follow the rule: flexibility first! Tables should, therefore, be square, rectangular, or trapezoidal since they are the most flexible. They can be combined for large groups, fitted into a corner, or lined up along a wall. Round or kidney-shaped tables steal space.

Both tables and chairs should be the proper size for the children using the room, chairs ten inches lower than the tables. Consult the chart on page 89 for specifications. Provide one chair for each child enrolled, with a few extra conveniently stored. Strong plastic chairs are durable, reasonable in cost, and available in colors. Since they are lightweight, they can easily be stacked and moved. Folding chairs are not recommended for children.

Bookshelves can double as room dividers and make access to art materials, games, and toys easy for children. Preschoolers need a slanting-shelf book case where the front of the books can be seen and enjoyed. The back of these units provide excellent storage space.

Bookrack

A bookrack, with slanted shelves on one side and flat shelves on the other, can serve the dual purpose of displaying books and providing shelf space for materials where children can reach them easily. It should be 42 to 46 inches high and 30 to 42 inches wide.

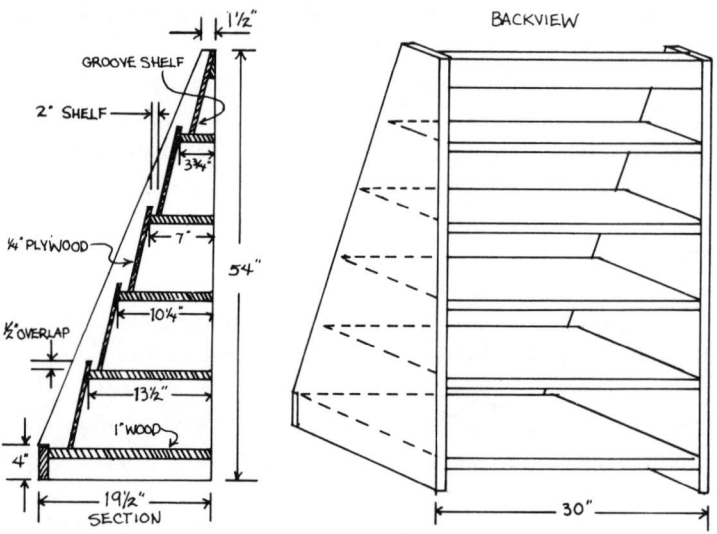

Used by permission of The Sunday School Board of the Southern Baptist Convention.

Storage

Shelf space should be provided for every group that uses the room. Cabinets with locking doors can be hung on the wall or built under a counter or sink. A clothes rack or coat hooks mounted under a shelf should also be standard equipment in any room used for children's church. Keeping children's coats, Bibles, and papers together can become a constant headache for second hour teachers. The coat rack or hooks and shelf should be mounted low enough for children to be responsible for their own belongings.

A welcome piece of equipment in a children's room is a unit including a sink, counter, and cupboard. This encourages creative activities by making cleanup easy and greatly reduces students' trips down the hall!

Musical Instruments

Children's departments should include a good piano, preferably of studio size. If you must use an old upright, do not despair. Many of them have better tone than some new pianos, and you can always paint them the same color as the walls to reduce their bulk. Preschool children sing well with an autoharp or guitar. Musical bells which the children can play themselves are inexpensive and especially suited to worship. Each room needs its own record player and albums.

Classroom Supplies

Needs will vary from one department to another, but certain supplies are essential to almost any children's class. They include the following: *Art materials*—Drawing paper, newsprint or butcher paper, construction paper, crayons, water colors, tempera paints, clay or play dough, paste, scissors, yarn. *Writing materials*—Good pencils with erasers, lined and unlined paper. *Teacher supplies*—Chalk, erasers, flannelboard and easel, marking pens, chart paper, large construction paper for bulletin boards, pencil sharpener, paper punch, stapler.

Sharing Expensive Equipment

Vital to every teaching program is a resource room from which teachers can borrow needed but expensive equipment. If your church has not had such a resource room in the past, now is a good time to begin. The resources will get maximum usage as they are shared by both Sunday school and children's church workers. Church boards often wince at the thought of purchasing audio-visual equipment, but many do not hesitate to equip their church kitchens with far more costly appliances.[5] A good case can be made that teaching the Bible is more important than preparing food!

Audio-visual equipment should include filmstrip and overhead projectors, puppets and a puppet stage, cassette recorders, and the software (filmstrips, tapes, transparencies, etc.) to go with this equipment. A portable listening station equipped with headgear so three to five children can listen to a story at once is a valuable tool. (See the Appendix section for information on making listening stations.) A file containing maps, pictures, flannel backgrounds, and Bible-time costumes should also be provided. Pop-up Bible storybooks and books with taped or recorded narrations crowd the shelves of any Christian bookstore. Purchase a selection, but be careful to read them first; some are inaccurate.

These media are not luxuries; they are the means by which this generation is learning vast amounts of trivia and secular knowledge every day. We handicap children's learning of truth if we fail to provide them for Christian education. Until your church can purchase its own equipment, ferret out what is available in your community. Public libraries lend projectors, filmstrips, and records. Motels which cater to clubs and conventions sometimes make their projectors available to the public. Ask a larger church if they are willing to share or rent their audiovisuals. Request of your own church that it find a dedicated, well-organized person who will make a ministry out of media. Do not give up until your resource room is a reality!

Improvements Anyone Can Make

Unless a church has just outfitted a new, fully equipped educational wing, teachers will probably find their rooms lacking some of the foregoing furnishings. That need not stop anyone from creating a good learning environment. Much can be done with homemade equipment. Fiberboard covered with bright burlap makes an excellent bulletin board. Carpet samples can be glued to an old rug for a warm and colorful new floor covering. Paint a windowless classroom a sunny yellow and create false "windows" to give an illusion of outdoors. Room too small? Scenic posters will push out the walls. Too large and impersonal? Curtains, area rugs, and low room dividers will warm it up.

If costs are your overriding concern, collect large cardboard cartons. All kinds of furniture—bookshelves, easels, tables and chairs—can be made from corrugated cardboard. In fact, two coats of chalkboard paint give it a good writing surface! For a more permanent chalkboard, put the paint on a length of Masonite.

Neighborhood garage sales practically give away toy furniture. They also offer card tables, file cabinets, and record players at low cost. Keep standards high—be sure furniture is in good condition—but do not overlook this inexpensive means of equipping your room.

As a leader, you need not do everything yourself. Find talented people in your church who will respond to the need. Most classroom furniture can be made by a weekend carpenter: challenge someone handy with tools to build a bookshelf or puppet stage. (For directions and designs for homemade equipment see the Appendix Section.) An electrician might delight to design an answer-board that lights up or rings a bell. Enlist a college student home for the summer to make a large wall map. Ask a few retirees to make hand puppets. Allow many of God's people to share in the privilege of equipping His sanctuary.

Imagine that you have just received your room location for this year's children's church program. Step back and look at the room you have inherited. Ask yourself, "If this were my home, would I be satisfied with its function and appearance? What can be done to make it more attractive? What does it need to be a better environment for learning and worship?"

We have been speaking of mundane matters—square feet and chair heights and cardboard furniture; but we began this chapter with an exalted theme, teaching the worship of the Lord God. That is the purpose served by the walls and furnishings we work to provide.

As Solomon dedicated the great temple in Jerusalem, he stated its purpose in his prayer that "all people of the earth may know thy name. . .that they may know that this house, which I have builded is called by thy name" (1 Kings 8:43). Does the room in which you and the children will worship evoke an awareness of God? Would a stranger, stepping through the door, know it speaks of Him? Your temple cannot be made of cedar, stone, and beaten gold as Solomon's was, but it can house something of eternal significance, an environment that is pleasing, functional, and stimulating, one in which a new generation can learn that which since ancient days has been the true worship of the Lord God.

Notes

1. Paul H. Vieth, *Worship in Christian Education* (Philadelphia: United Church Press), p. 13.
2. George Hedley, as quoted in Vieth, *When Protestants Worship*, p. 8.
3. Vieth, *Worship*, p. 8.
4. *The Standard* (Evanston: Harvest Publications, July-August 1979), p. 21.
5. Locke E. Bowman, Jr., *Straight Talk About Teaching in Today's Church* (Philadelphia: Westminister Press, 1967), p. 75.

Facility Standards

Department	Minimum sq. ft. per student	Recommended maximum students in department	Bulletin board & chalkboard height above floor	Chair height*
NURSERY	30' - 35'	15	20"	10"
BEGINNER	25' - 30'	20 - 25	20" - 24"	10" - 12"
PRIMARY	20' - 25'	30	24" - 28"	12" - 14"
JUNIOR	20' - 25'	30	30" - 32"	15" - 17"

*tables should be 10" above chairs

5

Preparing for Worship

The new teacher was visibly upset. The children in Primary Church I were behaving very badly. "Our snack time is atrocious! The children push and grab. They complain about the juice and never say thank you. We have to scold so much that no one's in the mood for worship. No matter what the book says, I have a good mind to give up refreshments altogether and start right in on the service!"

We sympathize with this harried teacher. All of us feel discouraged when the ideas that sound so rosy in the leader's guide work out less than perfectly in the classroom. The best solution is seldom the easy one—to drop the activity. Refreshments, rest, and relaxation are included in children's program guides not at the whim of an editor, but because children need them. In addition, the children's church program needs the opportunities they provide for fellowship and social exchange.

When well-planned activities do not run smoothly, teachers should remind themselves that the classroom is, after all, a microcosm of society. Each group represents a cross-section of personalities, spiritual levels, personal needs and interests. In each group interaction occurs among children and between children and adults. Personalities meet, mesh, and clash. Relationships develop, grow, and sometimes, deteriorate. Members, both child and adult, influence and affect one another.

In this microcosm of society opportunities for Christian living must take place. Children must see how Jesus affects the behavior of one person toward another. How does the teacher react when Johnny's juice spills on the floor—*again*? How do Christian children respond when a team member pulls a boner in a close game? Christian living must ensue before and after as well as during the worship service.

Meeting Children's Needs

The inset shows a figure that has helped people visualize how human needs affect behavior. Abraham Maslow's well-known hierarchy ranks universal needs in a simple pyramid, beginning with a human being's most elemental requirements and ascending to lofty heights of self-actualization and service to others.[1] Only as an individual's primary needs are met can he or she be free to operate on higher levels.

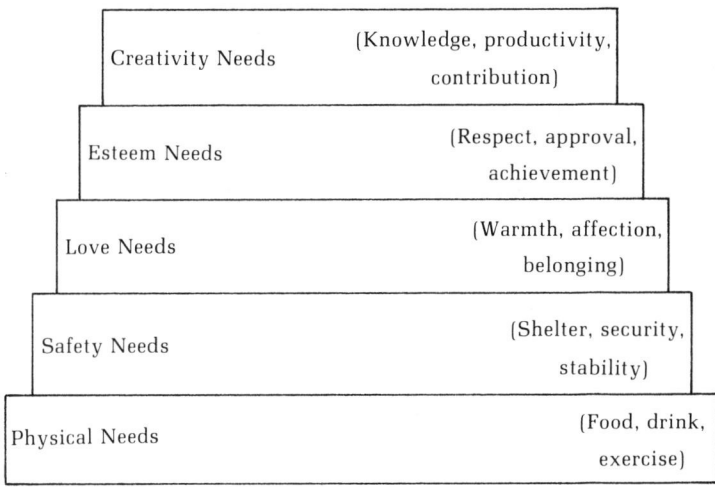

Hunger, thirst, and restlessness are manifestations of physical needs which dominate the attention even of adults. Children, however, require food, drink, exercise, and rest more often and more intensely. They cannot defer satisfaction for a considerable length of time, as adults can. Woe to the teacher who tries at 11:45 to teach the memory verse to children whose last nourishment was received at 7:45! Every teacher has experienced the "phidget phenomenon" that follows prolonged sitting. Children begin to fall off chairs, poke their buddies, scrape their feet—anything to satisfy those muscles shouting "Move!" The teacher may be concerned that the child's higher needs be met through learning God's Word, but at that moment his physical needs predominate, and he *cannot* attend to spiritual needs.

On a different level the child whose secure world is crumbling in divorce has little heart for learning, and the one who imagines his mother has abandoned him in the strange new world of children's church is deaf to your reassurances. In short, any time a child's basic needs are unmet, his energies and attention will tend to rivet on that need.

James tells us in no uncertain terms that it is wrong to try to minister to someone's spirit while ignoring his bodily needs: "If a brother or sister is without clothing and in need of daily food, and one of you says to them, 'Go in peace, be warmed and be filled,' and yet you do not give them what is necessary for their body; what use is that?" (James 2:15-16, NASB). Jesus always showed concern for His listener's physical welfare. He would not send a crowd of followers away hungry; He directed that the little girl He raised be fed immediately; He fixed breakfast one memorable morning for friends who had labored through the night.

With these biblical reminders that we minister to the whole person, we consider physical needs as well as lesson content when we plan the church time hour. Children's small stomachs empty quickly, so we include a light snack. Their active bodies tire easily, so we alternate periods of rest and movement. Young children feel threatened by sudden changes, strange faces, unfamiliar surroundings, so we plan for familiar routines and recruit a faithful staff.

Happily for us, God created us so that meeting our physical needs often helps nourish our spirits. Christian fellowship around the dinner table is as old as the Book of Acts and as recent as last Sunday after church. Sunday school picnics and church fun nights are evidence that we grow to know and love each other in play as well as in work and worship. With this in mind, we prepare to plan the first fifteen or twenty minutes of the children's church hour.

Plan a Smooth Transition

The first few minutes of a program can set the tone for the whole hour. Do not let the transition time from Sunday school to children's church become a no-man's-land of undefined responsibility. Arrange with the Sunday school department leaders the best way to move from one program to the next. One curriculum suggests that as Sunday school draws to a close, teachers gather the children for a song or finger play. The church time teacher takes over midway through the activity. Older children might complete worksheets or say memory verses as their transitional activity. If children must go to a different room for children's church, dismiss those who go home and have the rest follow you quietly to their new destination.

Relaxation

A good way to begin the hour for beginners and older children is to gather everyone for a circle game. Twos and threes will be happiest playing in the housekeeping center or block corner. Choose a game that allows large-muscle movement but not running. Old fashioned games like Hot Potato (Pretend an object is a hot potato. Pass it quickly from one to another until music stops. Whoever has it must drop out.), Walking Relays (Balance a chalkboard eraser on your head to the goal-line and back. First team done wins.), and Simon Says (if you keep it going fast) are still popular. To overcome the problem of having several "drop outs" waiting around instead of getting exercise, use the red tag system. All players wear red tags. Those who must drop out remove their tags but keep playing. Last red tag wins!

In addition to the old favorites, compile a list of games and keep them in a 3" x 5" card file. A list of books with directions for games are available in bookstores and your local library. Look for different kinds of games—quieting-down, get-to-know-you games, as well as get-the-wiggles-out types. You will find them lifesavers for those moments when the schedule has gone awry—a speaker is delayed or the handcraft is completed early—or for sultry, overcast days when everyone seems to need a break.

Rest for the Young Ones

After an hour or more of Sunday school twos, threes, and even fours need a few moments of rest. Records with quieting music help children settle down. Each child gets his own bath towel, mat, or pillow and stretches out on the floor. Turn out the lights and play the record or piano softly. After about five minutes, call the children a few at a time for the next activity.

Washroom for Everybody

Take young children to the washrooms at least once during the morning. Older children go by themselves during the transition or at game time. Remind them that there will be no interruptions during worship except in an emergency.

More Than a Word about Refreshments

Many programs include snacks as the first activity of the hour, but for several reasons it seems to work better after games. For one thing, teachers are spared the discomfort of serving snacks to children who stay for church time while other children, still waiting for parents to pick them up from Sunday school, look on. Secondly, and more important, refreshments can have a quieting effect if served properly. Eating provides time for the social amenities valuable to people who will worship together later.

Plan snack time as carefully as you do the rest of the hour. Here is opportunity for children to learn in a practical way that Christians think of God first, others next, themselves last. Unconsciously it may prepare them for a deeper experience of Christian communion, when one believer shares with another the symbolic bread.

Sit with the children around the table. Ask a child or teacher to offer a simple "Thank you, Lord, for this good snack." If food is served on a dish or tray, show them how to offer it first to their neighbor and then to help themselves. Say nothing about manners. Serving each other is simply Christian thoughtfulness in action.

Is it unrealistic to expect children of the 1980s to resist diving in and grabbing? Is not "Me first" the slogan of the school and playground? Yes, but we do not have to accept it! Work from the very first day to shape a new code of behavior. The way you serve the food can make a difference. I once observed a kind-hearted teacher make popcorn for a group of youngsters. The children waited with growing impatience while the aroma filled the room. When the corn finally popped, the teacher dumped it on a tray in the middle of the table. Normally well-behaved children threw themselves across the table to grab all they could! Serving it individually would have helped them control themselves.

Snacks should be reasonably nourishing and, when possible, correlated in some way with the theme. Many curriculum guides include suggestions for doing this. In addition to a glass of juice or water, serve crackers or some solid food. Try to avoid sweets or junk foods. Children love sliced fruit, vegetable sticks, graham crackers or crackers with cheese or peanut butter. All of the cost and preparation need not fall on the teachers. Some churches buy juice in quantity and ask teachers to arrange for snacks. Parents are usually happy to share in providing food if they are asked in advance and put on a rotating schedule.

Let children help you serve, then praise their efforts. Converse while you serve and eat together. This is the time to ask about family and friends, favorite activities, how the Little League team is doing. If children cannot seem to focus on anything but last night's TV horror flick, you carry the conversational ball. Start a round of questions like, "Where did you live when you were five years old and what kind of pet did you have?" Encourage teachers and children alike to share recent events in their lives. Stop to sing "Happy Birthday" to a celebrating child. Wrap things up after ten minutes or so, being sure that everyone finishes and cleans up his place. Teachers who are in charge of small group activities should now be at their tables, ready to begin the next part of the program.

Small Group Activities

After children are refreshed and relaxed they should be ready for a structured learning experience. In small, teacher-led groups children work on projects planned to further the worship aim. Some activities will be largely verbal, helping children develop new concepts of God, others will demand physical activity for role play or drama, still others will employ children's creative skills.

We should note here that some children's church programs schedule small group activities for *after* the worship time. Leaders of preschoolers find that they worship better earlier in the hour. With primaries and older, however, activities usually *precede* worship, since they often contribute to the service in some way. Children might, for example, prepare a puppet play around a Bible theme to present in the worship time or learn a new hymn to sing. Some teaching may be involved in the activity, as the small-group teacher expands on the Sunday school lesson or presents a new facet of truth; but the emphasis in small group activities is on discovery—the child acquires the concept or enlarges his understanding as he works through the planned project with his group.

Why Small Groups?

Church teachers sometimes ask, "Can't children learn effectively when the whole group is taught together? Isn't teaching everyone at once easier and more efficient? Why break up into small groups with the inevitable confusion and time-loss this entails?"

The reasons all boil down to one: Most children learn better that way. Children (and adults too) are more likely to participate when activities involve only a handful of people. They ask questions more frequently, respond to the leader more often, share personal feelings more freely. While there is no evidence to prove that small groups *learn greater quantities of information* than large groups do, there is evidence that the more deeply an individual is involved in the learning process, the more meaningful, and therefore permanent, will be his learning. Small groups encourage involvement.

For maximum interaction in your groups, keep numbers under eight. Studies show that groups of four to six generate better decisions, cooperate more satisfactorily, and solve problems faster than smaller or larger groups.[2]

Small Groups Foster Relationships

Nothing is more important to a child's learning than the nature of his relationship with the teaching adult. Relationships can be strengthened only in interpersonal exchange, as eye meets eye, hands touch in a common task, and voice responds to voice. This kind of dynamic interaction, fostered best in small groups, affects learning as surely as any curriculum or teaching method.

In addition to helping the learner, small groups help the teacher know where the student is. As they lead group activities, teachers can gain insight into each individual child's understandings. Instead of having to guess if listeners "got the idea" of the story, teachers observe whether Jeffrey can give an example of forgiveness, whether Doug can explain 1 John 1:9 in his own words, and whether Julie can illustrate it in a sketch. This kind of close evaluation is difficult, if not impossible, in large groups.

Small Groups Allow Planning for Worship

Worship is sometimes spoken of as if it were a show or program put on for people to watch. Nothing could be further from the truth. The philosopher Kierkegaard and many after him have recognized that in worship, the congregation, pastor, and choir are all participants, and *God* is the audience.[3] Our expressions of love, praise, and wonder are directed at Him, not each other. The worship "service" is a service to God.

Children learn this attitude toward worship as they work together to apply their talents and skills for participation in the service. When they practice for the rhythm band, design a stained-glass window, write a litany, or recite a psalm in chorus, they are following a biblical pattern for worship.

> Both the tabernacle and temple in their construction and maintenance depended on the many skills with which God had endowed His people. Professional musicians played and sang. . . . Worshippers and priests participated in the drama of sacrifice. . . . It pleases God for us to pour creative energy into our worship services and to use various forms of worship.[4]

No better time exists than childhood to develop habits of creative response to God. In teacher-led groups of five or six, children can plan and carry out significant portions of the worship time. They can learn a new song and sing it as a choir, prepare a frieze or mural for a focus of worship, prepare a shadow-puppet rendering of a Bible story.

In her book, *Children Can Worship,* Mary LeBar describes a worship hour with a group of juniors.[5] The theme for the morning focused on God's power. One group of children studied the creative power of God shown in water. They examined a drop under a microscope, listed the various forms water could take and discussed its value for man. Finally they painted a mural to illustrate all this. Another group studied the stars in a similar way. In the worship service later in the morning the mural was displayed. The children in group two stood near it and interspersed facts they had learned about the universe with appropriate Scripture verses. A third group interviewed

Bible characters whose lives revealed the power of God, and a fourth group sang "How Great Thou Art." God's power was convincingly portrayed by the youngsters and celebrated in corporate worship. By their expression of praise, they led others to praise Him, too.

Activities Build Concepts

Small group activities deepen and clarify understandings. Children do not easily bridge the gap between concrete images and abstract ideas implicit in many Bible passages. Children need help, for example, in applying the metaphor "The Lord is my Shepherd" to their own lives. Even after doing research on shepherds and sheep, after building a small sheepfold, or arranging a fuzzy flock "beside the still waters" of a sandbox, children have to translate this into: God takes care of me when I'm alone in the dark; He plans my life and supplies everything I need and more; He is to me what the Shepherd is to the sheep. It takes many different kinds of experiences for children to begin to comprehend this spiritual truth.

One morning our small group activities centered on the theme of showing mercy—a difficult concept for primaries to grasp. They accepted our explanation and the example we gave of mercy's being "kindness to someone who doesn't deserve it."[6] It then became their task to make up a flannel-figure story of someone showing mercy. They were soon busy devising intricate scenes and figures and a simple plot: While Mom and Dad are out shopping, their children work hard to surprise them with a cleaned-up house. At that point one of the girls appealed to me. "The story's not right, is it? I know there's something wrong but I don't know what it is!" The girls looked from me to each other and back to the flannelboard. I could see the mental wheels turning as they struggled to distinguish mercy from other

Christian attributes—kindness, love, justice. "Yes," I agreed, "there is something wrong. Think about it. How could you make this story show *mercy*?" The girls were forced to rethink the definition and come up with a better example, which they did. This new plot was presented later during worship. Had these girls not had to come up with their own illustration of the concept "mercy," they would not truly have learned it, even though, as attentive and good students, they might have been able to parrot the definition.

Understanding through a first-hand or simulated experience is the great value of learning activities. A concept that the child receives can be sorted out, elaborated, illustrated, and expressed. In the process the concept becomes her own, one that will enrich her understanding of God and His works, one that will provide fuel for the fires of worship.

Choosing Activities

Sometimes children's activities are defended for reasons of "holding children's attention" or "keeping little hands busy." These are unworthy reasons for including them in children's church. Activities-for-activities'-sake constitutes an unjustifiable use of precious time. Besides, it is unnecessary. Children do not need to be entertained to be kept interested. Good learning activities capitalize on children's natural desire to learn. Caring teachers who stay up nights planning learning activities do it not merely to "hold the kids' attention,"—a policeman or a TV cartoon can do that—but to use the learning activities to *teach*. God made children so that they learn not only with their eyes and ears, but with their hands, noses, muscles, and glands. The more senses and sinews that are engaged, the stronger will be the learning.

If you are not convinced of that, think of the things you learned with your muscles—riding a bike, driving a car, playing "Chopsticks" on the piano. These learnings are never forgotten. So with Bible truths; children need to work them and walk them into their lives; they need to respond to them with their whole bodies if they are to learn them forever.

Criteria for Choosing Activities

We have talked so much about "good" learning activities on these pages that it is fair to ask, "What makes a good learning activity? What are the criteria by which activities should be chosen?" Below are listed eight characteristics of educationally sound activities. For simplicity's sake, we will call them the ABCs of choosing activities.[7]

The best learning activities—
- A - Assure personal expression. The child should not be able merely to copy or repeat the learning. He should have to filter it through his own personality and thought processes in the course of the activity.
- B - Bear upon life outside the church. How will the biblical command to think of others before oneself affect my behavior on the playground tomorrow?
- C - Correlate with age-level interests and abilities. Activities should reflect the family and cultural backgrounds of the children, as well as reflect their social, mental, and physical development.
- D - Deepen understanding of the concepts, values, and implications of the lesson.
- E - Employ as many of the senses as possible. Seeing slides of sheep and hearing a tape of their

bleating is vivid; but rubbing one's hands through the curly fleece and smelling the soft hide makes the experience unforgettable. A lesson that leads the student to listen, talk, observe, write, *and* manipulate materials is more likely to reach the objective because it travels so many roads to learning.

F - Foster creative effort. "The sensitive teacher says enough to start the children thinking, but not so much that thought is not necessary. He or she leaves enough freedom within the assignment for their initiative and inventiveness, requiring that the students hunt, think, and work."[8]

G - Grow directly from the Bible theme and are related to its significant meanings. A planter made from a coffee can is a nice handcraft, but it is probably not a learning-for-worship activity.

H - Hint at enough novelty to engage a reluctant learner. Children do not have to be dazzled with unique projects every week, but they do tire of activities that come up too often. Look for new ideas or find interesting ways to adapt old favorites. If children are to draw pictures illustrating a story, instead of the usual manila paper, give each a sheet of fine sandpaper. By crayoning hard they will obtain dramatic colors. Get a bonus copy by placing the sandpaper over construction paper and pressing with a warm iron. *Of course,* let the children do it—with your supervision.

Planning Activities

You have assessed and chosen activities, collected

materials, and you are ready to prepare for Sunday morning. How can you be sure the activity is going to work? Four steps are important in the planning process.

1. Be clear about objectives. What, exactly, do you want to be the outcome of this activity? What should the child be able to do as a result of it? Your leader's guide should, but may not, include objectives (or aims) for the student's learning. If it does, you may have to revise the objectives to fit your children's special needs. If the leader's guide does not specify objectives, write them yourself—they are worth the trouble. Remember that an objective states *what the child will be able to do,* not what the teacher is going to do. Many teachers find it helpful to follow this formula: "As a result of this activity, students should be able to. . . ." (Define the meaning of the word blessed; give an example of God's power working in David's life; write an original song of praise; or whatever.) Do not fall into the trap of stating objectives in vague, too-general terms like, ". . .the student will be able to understand that Jesus is our Shepherd." Instead state a specific response that will help you determine *how well* he understands: ". . .the student will write a haiku poem showing one way Jesus is like a Shepherd."

2. Do a sample of the activity. Doing it yourself helps you work the bugs out and gives confidence as you motivate the children. It is not always a good idea to show your sample to the children—that sometimes stifles creativity—but you will benefit from working through it.

3. Think through procedures. Walk through the activity mentally, step by step, as the children will do it. Where will the children be when you explain

the activity? What kind of motivation will be needed? How will materials be dispensed? Where will the children work? How long should each part of the activity take? How will you (or *will* you) guide and direct conversation during the activity? How will the children share their product or experience? Try to anticipate problems that may arise, then revise your plans accordingly.

When using art materials, keep directions as brief as possible. Always explain procedures first, then give out materials. Nothing is more frustrating to a child than having to listen to teacher's lengthy directions with the crayons already in his hot little hands!

4. Evaluate afterwards. Finally, as soon after children's church as possible, evaluate the activity. How many children achieved the objective? Did the learning contribute significantly to worship? Is the activity sufficiently worthwhile to be used again? How could it be improved? Evaluation is a most important step, especially on those Sundays when the activity fizzled! Your morale will improve immediately as you begin to determine just what went wrong and how it can be corrected next time.

This chapter has dealt with the fellowship and small group activities that occur in the first part of the children's church hour. The next chapter will outline specific activities teachers can employ in helping children learn to worship. The worship time itself, usually climaxing the hour, will be discussed in Chapter 7.

Notes

1. A. H. Maslow's theory, adapted from Thorpe and

Schmuller, *Personality; An Interdisciplinary Approach* (Princeton: Van Nostrand, 1958), pp. 49-51.

2. J. M. Lee, *The Flow of Religious Instruction* (Mishawaka: Religious Education Press, 1973), p. 67.

3. "Power, Preaching & Priorities," *Leadership* (Winter 1980), p. 21.

4. D. C. Smith, *Worship Service Planner* (Elgin: David C. Cook Publishing Co., Summer 1978), p. 4.

5. Mary LeBar, *Children Can Worship* (Wheaton: Victor Books/Scripture Press, 1976), p. 106.

6. This activity is included in Gospel Light's *Growing in God's Family Church Time Leader's Guide,* p. 62.

7. Adapted and expanded from E. Jeep, *Classroom Creativity* (New York: Herder and Herder, 1970), p. 10.

8. Ibid., p. 10.

6

Activities for Learning and Worship

"The teacher is the nerve center of the instructional process," says religious educator James Michael Lee. From the teacher's knowledge of her students and from her repertoire of teaching/learning strategies must emerge those which will help learning happen in these particular students at this particular time. As the nerve center, the teacher needs to develop not only a large number but also a balanced variety of learning activities—those that employ all the different senses and capabilities of the child. No teacher ever has enough of these activities, and no book can encompass more than a sampling of them. Those included here are meant to assist teachers in diversifying their approach to meet children's changing needs.

Categories of Activities

Teaching/learning strategies can be categorized in any number of ways. Usually they are listed under headings like Art Activities, Drama, Written Assignments, or Discussion. Most of us tend to prefer one kind over another—Teacher A is strong on art activities, Teacher B likes learning games and puzzles, Teacher C uses lots of discussion and sharing. In order for teachers to have a built-in check on the balance of learning activities they are providing, the activities are categorized here according to how much of the child's whole person is engaged in the activity: Physical (whole body), Manipulative (handling objects and materials), Creative (art and music), and Verbal (written and oral). To remind us that the learning of biblical concepts, principles, and behavior necessarily involves cognition, or mental activity, the word *Mental* is included in each title. The younger the child, the greater the importance of the physical and intuitive domains over the cognitive. As children mature, verbal experiences increase in importance, though not as much as our overuse of them in class would indicate.

Undeniably, the divisions are somewhat arbitrary; categories do overlap and interplay—writing a song, for example, is obviously both verbal and creative! Since, however, the creative element is most essential to the outcome, the activity is placed in that category.

Modes of Learning

As the teacher designs and uses activities for all these categories he or she succeeds in touching each child in several ways, and, what is perhaps more important, in activating each child's special mode of learning. Some children learn best through creative projects; others learn visually and kinesthetically; a smaller number learn best through the spoken or printed word.

Recent discoveries about the differences between the right and left hemispheres of the brain underline the importance of knowing each student's dominant mode of learning. Children whose left brain hemispheres dominate respond better to verbal, analytical, and logical learning activities; those who are predominantly right-brained learn best through visual and creative experiences. But for all children, learning is increased when *both* hemispheres of the brain are involved.

Nonverbal vs. Verbal Activities

Children need rich experiences with the nonverbal activities outlined under categories A, B, and C, if they are to handle the verbal learnings of category D meaningfully. Although church and secular teaching have emphasized verbal presentation, educational research reveals that children (and adults, for that matter) seldom learn by words alone. One authority in the field, David Ausebel, said flatly that for children the grasping of abstract ideas "must always be preceded by an adequate background of direct, nonverbal experience" with the idea.[1]

The abstract concept *grace,* for example, will be better and earlier understood by adolescents who as children experienced the forgiving love of parents and teachers they wronged, felt the wonder of God's mercy for sinners through Bible dramatizations, and expressed their feelings in music, movement, and other nonverbal ways.

What this means for us is that we need to enlarge greatly our use of the first three categories of learning strategies—Mental-Physical, Mental-Manipulative, and Mental-Creative, while providing better and more effective Mental-Verbal activities.

Mental-Physical Learning Activities

Our three-year-old visitor was giving us an animated account of his new kitten's antics. "He go'th under th' table and hide'th and he jumpth out at you and he wunth away!" With every rushing word Jeremy made a corresponding action—he climbed under the table, jumped, waved his arms and ran in circles, just as the kitten he was describing. It was as necessary for Jeremy to act out an event as it was for him to talk about it.

Young children require constant opportunities to learn

with their whole bodies. As children mature, action-oriented learning continues to be important, although it plays a lesser role.

Playacting

Playacting is a whole-body activity vital to the learning and development of young children. A prime center for playacting is the homemaking center, where preschoolers spontaneously or with guidance act out the lessons they are learning about Christian behavior. "I'll help you put the dishes away," says Amy, helping her friend. Timmy resolves a conflict amicably with the suggestion, "O.K., you can be the Daddy this time, and I'll be the Daddy next time." These are enactments of the Scripture they are using repeatedly, "Be kind to one another." The teacher sets up classroom opportunities to practice life truths in these concrete ways by bringing the lesson into the play experience: "We all need to cook our food, but there is only one pot. What shall we do?"

In addition to furniture, the play area includes dress-up clothes that help children portray familiar roles. A golf or fishing cap for Father, purse and necklace for Mother, a lunch box for Sister to take to school. For depicting Bible stories, a crown, helmet, and shepherd's headdress are available. A rectangular length of cloth with a hole cut in the middle and a sash provide Bible time attire for any number of roles.

Prepare children to act out the Bible story in worship time. When telling the story of David, have one boy dressed up and stationed behind a door or screen. At the right moment call David "in from the fields," to be anointed by Samuel. Two girls will delight to play Miriam and Pharoah's daughter tenderly caring for Moses at the riverside.

Playacting is especially suited to church time because it is an ideal way to review and deepen the understanding of a story. Children take their roles seriously and with very little guidance are able to act out the story, reliving it in the process.

Echo-Pantomine

In this simple form of drama everyone gets into the act! Echo-Pantomine does not require costumes and can be performed by everyone in concert. It should follow an earlier presentation of the story. The teacher explains that children are to "echo" the teacher's words by appropriate actions. After she says a line of the story the children (and other teachers) respond with the motions. For example:

> "David went and hid behind a big rock." (Children crouch to hide.)
>
> "He looked across the field for Jonathan." (Shade eyes and peer into distance.)
>
> "Soon Jonathan came with his big bow and arrow." (Stand tall, holding up arm.)
>
> "He shot an arrow way, way, across the field!" (Aim and let fly!)
>
> "David waved to his good friend." (Wave goodbye.)
>
> "And ran as fast as he could off into the hills." (Run in place.)
>
> "Jonathan prayed that God would protect his friend." (Bow in prayer.)

Role Play

Role play has a different purpose from other forms of dramatization and is most effective with older children. In role play the child takes on the role of a character in a story and behaves as he thinks the character would. There is no script or rehearsal. The purpose is to stand in another's shoes and feel as he feels—something children must learn to do as they mature. Role play helps them understand the emotional content of Bible stories and can also provide opportunities to determine ways Christians should respond to everyday problems.

To use role play, describe a true-to-life situation and assign roles to students. Try *not* to assign them to those whose personalities mirror the character's—for example, do not ask the aggressive boy in your class to role play a bully. Set the stage with minimal props, and let the action proceed. The following is a role play that might be used with middler or junior children.

"Doug's class is having a social studies test. Doug studied and is doing O.K., but his friend Stephen keeps pestering him. As usual, Stephen did not study, and now he wants Doug to let him copy. Doug pretends not to hear him. Finally, to make Doug turn around, Stephen throws a rubber eraser at him. The teacher sees it and jumps up. 'Are you two copying? Come up here this minute!'"

Ask three children to finish the scene. Explain that Doug is a Christian, and Stephen is his best friend. Ask the audience to listen carefully and be ready to discuss the participants' behavior. Let the role play continue for three to five minutes, depending on the action, then call it to a halt. "Debrief" each player by asking him how he felt as the character and why he acted as he did. Discuss with the audience their feelings about the problem and whether alternate solutions could be found. Sometimes it is beneficial to repeat the role play, using other players. Remember these steps when using role play:

1. Describe the situation, problem, or dilemma.
2. Assign players. Encourage but do not insist if a child is reluctant to participate.

3. Review the situation and tell participants a little bit about their characters, particularly what their attitude is—angry, cheerful, interested, discouraged, or whatever.
4. Tell the audience what to listen for.
5. Set the stage and let action proceed 3-5 minutes.
6. "Debrief" players.
7. Elicit reactions and conclusions from the audience.

Role play can be used in creative ways. Let children make up and act out role plays illustrating a Bible verse. Let them make up one for other children to act out or let them do the same one several times, showing optional behaviors.

Informal Skits and Puppet Plays

For informal skits and puppet plays children can devise a script and act out a very familiar story. Children too young to write can receive extra help from teachers. As the children rehearse the plot, repeating what they remember of the character's words, teachers can write down or tape record the dialogue. Later the children can perform the skit or puppet play during the worship service.

Middlers and juniors enjoy staging a skit behind a shadow screen. Even shy children will usually participate in this form of drama in which they are protected from the direct gaze of the audience. Hang a white sheet in front of a light and darken the room. Actors stand directly behind the sheet.

Primaries and younger children love puppets, perhaps because controlling a smaller person gives them a chance to be the big people, for a change! For one quarter our primaries had studied events in Jesus' life. As a culminating activity, we asked them to choose from among selected Bible characters one to make as a hand puppet.

After a couple weeks of cutting, gluing and decorating felt, we had King Herod with an ugly frown, the Samaritan woman with dangly earrings, and other equally graphic renditions of New Testament personages. We grouped children according to their stories and helped each group "write" a brief script. We made copies of the scripts and taped them on the inside of the puppet stage (a table turned on its side), where children could easily read the parts. They performed the plays as the Bible message for our worship time and later for a younger department.

Walk-Through Activities

Another way to involve the learner's whole body is to devise walking activities. These can be done in or out of doors and are limited only by the teacher's imagination. Any classroom floor can be turned into a walk-on map. Lay masking tape the length of the room, forming an outline of the Holy Land. Cut out and tape blue construction paper in the shape of the Dead Sea and Galilee, with the Jordan River snaking between. Have children help you locate the cities and towns you are studying in their proper places on the floor. To add color and interest, suspend from the ceiling posters and large pictures of scenes from the Holy Land hung above their probable locations. Sit on the map for activities, occasionally "sending" students from Jericho to Jerusalem, from Dan to Beersheba, and so forth.

Take younger children on a "Walk-through" of a familiar biblical event. To deepen impressions and review highlights of a unit on Moses, we had a Walk-through of the Exodus. We chose a Moses and gave him the only real prop—a staff. We explained that the church building (except the sanctuary full of worshipers) would become our Wilderness, and we must find our way out of Egypt and toward the Promised Land. We would leave our shoes in the classroom and walk softly on the desert sand (carpeted floors). Because the Egyptians were behind us we walked quickly through the hall, though not too quickly for the "babies" and "old people." Finally we reached the Red Sea (a large room with doors on each end). Moses extended his staff, the waves rolled back, and we stepped across the dry sea floor, marvelling all the way. When we grew thirsty in the Wilderness Moses struck a rock (water fountain), and we all took a drink. Back in the classroom we found "manna" in the form of candied popcorn neatly laid on napkins on the floor, and sat down to thank God and feast after our long trip. It was an activity children often asked us to repeat.

Mental-Manipulative Activities

The second category focuses on activities which require the manipulation of objects and materials. Children enjoy and need manipulative activities. They love to do finger plays, put puzzles together, play board games, feel interesting objects. Educational research indicates that acting on objects is an essential step in children's learning of concepts, particularly when the concept is new and unfamiliar. A *sandbox* where story figures can be moved around is a concrete way children can experience Abraham's sharing of the land with Lot. He understands the story better as he manipulates the figures himself. Older children benefit in a similar way as they move players on a *game board* from Jerusalem to Caesarea and on to Rome. A *bulletin board* can be a manipulative device as children place words or pictures under their proper classification or group. Have children, for example, classify pictures of Bible foods, plants, and animals, or names of New Testament writers, Old Testament writers, disciples, and prophets by placing them in the correct box.

A bulletin board can also serve as a giant game board for Bible Concentration or Bible Jeopardy.

A *time line* allows the manipulation of figures to help clarify Bible chronology. Hang a clothesline across the room; then have children arrange dates and pictures or symbols of Bible events in their historical order.

Much learning early in life takes place through the sense of touch. Young children learn as they feel and hold five smooth stones like the ones David used, or caress some silky, shiny cloth like that from which Queen Esther's dress was made. Make touch-and-feel pictures by gluing cloth and other material on figures in the scene. When teaching primaries a new Bible word, cut the letters out of sandpaper or velvet and glue them on a card for children to feel as well as see. When reviewing memory verses, write them with white crayon on a large white index card. Have children try to "read" them with their fingers. Then let them brush across the card with water color—words will appear like magic.

Manipulative devices are not hard to create once you begin consciously to make the effort. Captured by the pleasure of touch and the power of manipulation, children seldom realize how much and how permanently they are learning. For a small investment of money, good Bible board games can be purchased in Christian bookstores. For a larger investment in time and effort, create games and other manipulative devices especially suited to your program and your students' needs. Books listed in the Appendix supply ideas and directions.

Mental-Creative Activities

In the marred image of God which remains stamped on every human being few traces of Godlikeness are more discernable than the creative impulse. Within the limits of his finiteness man shapes, forms, designs, constructs, and beautifies his environment. And he finds deep satisfaction, when, like his Creator he can look on his work and see that it is good.

The creative impulse spans all ages and levels of intelligence. In children it is less inhibited and therefore more spontaneous than in adults. Because creativity seems to be located in the right brain hemisphere, children who have poor reading and writing skills may nevertheless be highly creative. A dextrous child may do beautiful things with art media; a musical child, with rhythm and instruments. Others will express creativity best in thought and word. All creative streams should be tapped in learning-for-worship activities.

Art

Dogs are born swimmers. Throw Bowser into the lake, and he will come up paddling every time. Children are born artists. They take to paint, clay, and crayons like a pup takes to water. Art media are powerful weapons in the teacher's arsenal of learning activities.

Painting: Church teachers may be afraid of paint—one seldom sees a paint easel or displays of children's paintings in Sunday school rooms. Yet no medium is more suited to the young child than tempera, large brushes, and sheets of newsprint. The results are boldly, beautifully satisfying. To allay teachers' fears of uncontrolled swishing, dripping, and mess, the following procedure is recommended.

Use a table instead of easels. (Less dripping!) Work with two to four children at a time—no more. Cover the table with plastic or newspapers, also the floor. Anchor paint jars or juice cans with lids in a paint tray in the center of the table—one tray for two children, two large brushes in each color. Use only the three primary colors—red, blue, and yellow. For older children, add brown and white. With these, children will blend exciting new colors on their paper. Provide no water; if brushes must be cleaned, use paper towels. Teach children a few simple procedures and stick to them: scrape excess paint on the edge of the jar; always put brushes back in the same color; work only on your paper; wear a smock (man's shirt with sleeves cut short, buttoned backwards). When painting must end for the morning, brushes should be soaked in a can of cold water. If you are fortunate enough to have a sink in your room, teach children to rinse brushes and stand them upright. Paintings can be left to dry on the table. Display them later at the worship center or have children interpret paintings to the group. Always find something to praise in children's paintings—the use of color, originality, or broad, clean strokes. Accept the child's effort as more important than the product.

Object printing: Tempera paints also come in handy for sponge printing and object printing. Small pieces of sponge or any number of household objects print interesting patterns when dipped in a little paint. Gift wrapping can be made this way, or backgrounds for the bulletin board. Make a star-studded night sky for a Christmas backdrop by printing with a cookie cutter. For vegetable prints, carve Christian symbols or other designs on a potato half. Dab in bright colors to decorate bookmarks, scrap books, or manuscript scrolls containing Scripture passages.

Murals and Friezes: A mural is a wall-size portrayal of a scene or event; a frieze is a series of panels showing different scenes of the same event. A mural can be an effective large-group project. Two children can design the background scene, working directly on the mural paper which teachers have hung on the wall. Tempera paint or colored chalk works well for the background. If you use paint, tape newspaper to the floor and walls near the mural. Give the rest of the children drawing paper so they can crayon or paint the people, animals, and buildings to complete the scene. These they cut out and paste on the mural—small ones in the distance, large ones near the front or lower part of the scene.

For a frieze, have one or two children work on each panel, then mount them side by side. Caution children to check each other's work to try to keep figures approximately the same size.

Triptych: These small, three-paneled altar pieces, often ornate and bejeweled, were designed for the churches and cathedrals of Europe. Now many grace the finest museums in the world. To create their own triptych, children could portray three scenes of a Bible story on poster board stock. These can be cut in rectangles or gothic arch shapes. Paint, heavy crayoning, or torn tissue paper make effective media for a triptych. A collage effect can be rendered by gluing bits of felt, yarn, twigs, or pebbles on the scene. Hinge the panels with scotch tape and stand to display.

Stitchery: When planning creative projects, do not forget stitchery. Children produce colorful banners and interesting wall hangings with a length of loosely woven cloth such as burlap, colorful yarn, and large-eyed needles. Introduce stitchery to young children with a simple project. Have them crayon or paint a picture on a large card, then punch holes in an interesting pattern around the picture. Let them lace through the holes with yarn taped at one end to keep it from unraveling.

Older children produce artistic gems with needle and thread. Recently a middler class created wall-hangings like the ones described below. Contrary to teachers' fears, none of the boys protested. In fact, they proved very capable and were proud of their work.

Have children sew colorful wall-hangings depicting familiar Christian symbols—a Cross, Fish, Shepherd's Crook, Dove; or, at Christmas, a Candle, Star, Angel, or Manger. Give each a burlap or muslin rectangle with an inch or wider hem at the top. They sketch simple outlines in chalk, then stitch with a contrasting yarn. If hangings are large, run a dowel through the hem and have the children attach yarn for a hanger. If they are small, a drinking straw will substitute for the dowel. These can be hung in the worship area and changed with the seasons of the church year.

Music

Make music big in your plans for learning activities! Music touches the emotions as nothing else can. For that reason alone, music is important for the children's church program. The emotional response so essential to worship can early be associated with Bible truths and church experiences as feelings are touched and expressed through music.

Instruments: Every room should have instruments children can play. Rhythm band instruments are standard, but others are valuable as well. Try to provide an auto harp, zither, xylophone, or Melode' Bells. Children old enough to read can follow a chart to show them which notes to play for favorite songs. Melode' Bells are especially good for preschoolers. They consist of a set of eight handbells in the key of F. The bells are numbered and color coded, so it is easy to make charts using corresponding colors which help youngsters play the tune. They can play a call to worship or accompany a song.

Writing Songs: Early in their lives children make up their own songs spontaneously. They love to repeat the same lines over and over, swaying as they sing. Employ this fleeting gift in the service of worship. Help children make up meaningful words to a well-known tune. Simple lines can be sung to the tune of "Mulberry Bush," for example: "Jesus said He'll never leave, never leave, never leave us, Jesus said He'll never leave, He's always, always, with us!"

One Easter morning a group of third graders discussed Christ's death and Resurrection. They looked at pictures of Golgotha and the garden tomb; they each tasted a dab of vinegar. They read John 20 together and talked about Mary's joy when Jesus found her in the garden and of Thomas's problems with doubt. Then the teacher led them in a song-writing session. Playing the familiar tune of "Michael Row the Boat Ashore," she asked them to think through the chapter again. They were to make up one line about each part of the story, ending in words of praise. She showed them how to fit the words to the rhythm. Later they would sing it for worship. This is what they wrote:

"Who will roll the stone away? Halleluia!

It is gone—where is my Lord? Halleluia!

They looked in the tomb for Christ—He was risen!

It was hard to believe, but He showed them His scars.

Jesus said, Peace to you, I am Risen!

Jesus said, Peace to you, I am Risen!"

They performed their new hymn as a choir, singing lustily. It was the climax of a meaningful Resurrection service.

Creative Writing

Creative writing is usually thought of as a verbal activity, as indeed it is. However, the essential ingredients in truly creative writing are originality and imagination—intuitive, right-brain activities rather than logical, left-brain ones. The teacher should strive to elicit vivid, graphic images from the children and help them convey these images in poetry and prose. Even preschoolers can do this. To capture permanently the imaginative thoughts of young children, show them a picture of a Bible event—perhaps one of Jesus and a group of children. Activate their minds with questions about what they see and write down their responses. Later on a chart under the picture, write their words to be read aloud often.

Children of five and over write delightful poetry. After a child makes a picture or painting, talk with him about writing a short poem to go with it. Even kindergarteners understand that language has rhythm, and they enjoy making rhymes (though that is not essential to poetry). The child's poem can be written under the picture and shared in the worship service.

Write a Psalm: Can children write psalms? Some of our teachers were skeptical about this activity suggested in our children's church curriculum.[2] They could not imagine some of our active middlers getting excited about psalm-writing. But write psalms they did, not only the naturally verbal children, but the rowdiest of the lot.

First we talked about David and his lonely night vigils in the fields and caves of Judea. We talked about the wild animals he feared and the sky and stars that he loved. We read a few of his lines of praise to a powerful, protecting Lord. Then we asked what each of the children admired about God. They wrote down their thoughts. Jeff, a visitor who had never before been in church and could not write well, dictated his psalm to the teacher.

> God, how do you do all those wonderful things that you do?
>
> You do them because you are so great!

Christine, a sensitive nine-year-old, wrote this:

> Wonderful is the Lord, I will thank Him for His goodness.
>
> He has loved me in my sin.

He knows my every thought and He loves me.
His ways are holy.
The Lord has died for me so I can live for Him.
Praise the Lord! I will praise Him for His goodness.

But it was Sherri's psalm that dampened the eyes of teachers during the worship program.

Thank you for all them prayers you answer, Lord.
Thank you for all them things you do for us. . . .
And we all love you, Lord.

Mental-Verbal Activities

Tell me—I'll forget.
Show me—I'll remember,
Walk with me—I'll understand.

Most teachers know by now that the poorest way to learn something is to listen to someone else talk about it. We know that strictly verbal teaching methods seldom have the impact that visual and enactive methods do. Even so, the preponderance of learning activities church teachers plan for children tend to fall in the strictly verbal category—listening, talking, reading, and writing. And that is understandable. After all, the great truths of the Christian faith are abstract ideas like love, trust, redemption, and immortality. Ultimately, they must be expressed verbally!

As a result, Christian teachers struggle to broaden and deepen their scope of verbal learning activities. Partly in response to teacher demand, curriculum guides and teaching magazines offer a changing menu of ideas for stimulating discussions, planning research projects, writing newspapers, diaries, scrapbooks, and Scripture paraphrases. All these are excellent methods. Directions for using them can be found in current books and periodicals listed in the Appendix. The following verbal teaching-learning methods are especially suited to children's church, and belong in any teacher's repertoire.

Guided Converstaion: Teachers of preschoolers will recognize this method. It is one that must be mastered by teachers of the very young, but should be used (though somewhat more subtly) with older children as well. It requires that teachers be free of secretarial or other duties so they can converse with children as they play or work.

In guided conversation the teacher gently directs the children's thoughts toward the Bible theme of the morning. He or she does this by joining children as they play at the block corner or color at a table or serve tea in the play kitchen. The teacher asks questions and plants thoughts that will lead the child to consider the implications of a Bible truth.

Guided conversation often takes place in the course of another planned activity. For example, one morning the emphasis was on sharing. The aim was to have each child experience one activity in which he must share. The children had a choice of three learning activities: making a free-form picture, helping to make a bulletin board, or preparing a special snack. At each center supplies were deliberately limited. Children had to decide how to work together, sharing tools and materials. While no child was able to do all the activities, each was exposed to a sharing situation. During this time teachers guided their conversation as necessary. They talked with them about sharing and how it fit in with the message from God's Word to "Do that which is right and good." At one of the centers children sang a sharing song as they worked. They spent a happy morning learning experientially what it means to "do that which is right and good."[3]

Case Study: School-age children need to talk. They need to share with understanding adults the conflicts and stresses which occur every day in their young lives. Somehow, church classes seldom provide the right opportunities.

The case study is a problem-solving technique which has helped children, youth, and adults to express their concerns, questions, and feelings about the Christian life. It is especially suited to children eight or older. A case study is a short story from real life involving a central individual and how he handled a problem. It differs from a simple illustration in that the group itself discusses the case and makes a decision about the outcome. In the process they sort out and clarify their own responses to the problem.

Since learners must be able to identify closely with the person and recognize the problem as an authentic one, choose the story carefully. Select it from your own personal experience, if possible, or from the lives of children you know. If you have little contact with children outside of class, watch the newspapers for episodes and check out children's books and magazines from your local library. If you can stand it, force yourself to watch some of the TV shows your children like. Choose an incident that relates closely to the Bible principle you are studying. Decide whether to present it orally or on a handout and whether to relate the whole episode or stop short of the solution. In the former case, ask the children to evaluate the individual's solution. Was it a wise one? Would you have done it that way? Why or why not? In the latter case, after presenting the situation, ask, "What would *you* do in this case?" Lead the children to examine all the influencing factors in the case—the individual's background, age, circumstances, and personality. Help them to apply the biblical principle. Ask them how this kind of situation compares to their own experience at home or school. Keep questions open, avoiding those that can be answered Yes or No, except as a lead-in to, "Why do you say that, John?" or "How would *you* handle it, Jenny?"

If the case study falls flat, find out why. Try another one, and this time record the discussion on tape. As you listen to yourself, ask, "Are my questions open and probing? Do I tend to answer them myself, or do I really give learners time to respond?" Most teachers do not, according to a recent study. Waiting just three seconds or longer will reap a larger harvest of responses.[4] Correct mistakes in your next attempt. In time, you will find case study an excellent way to encourage children to discuss issues that are important to them.

Choral Speaking: Speech choirs are an ancient and effective means of fusing thoughts and words to expression for worship. Even young children can do simple forms of choral speech. During activity time, have a small group work in a choral reading of a Scripture passage. Use solo lines, duets, and choral responses as you would in a choir number. Guide the children to see that certain words should be emphasized (older children can choose these themselves); that voices should now drop to a whisper, now crescendo; that certain lines should be repeated or echoed. In the process, children begin to "feel" the passage in a fresh way. Here is a sample of choral speech for Psalm 148, NIV.

Praise the Lord.	All
Praise the Lord from the heavens,	
Praise him in the heights above.	
Praise him, all his angels,	Girls
Praise him, all his heavenly hosts.	Boys
Praise him, sun and moon,	Solo
Praise him, all you shining stars.	Solo
Praise him, you highest heavens	Boys
And you waters above the skies....	Girls
Praise the Lord from the earth,	All
You great sea creatures and all ocean	

    depths,
Lightening and hail, snow and clouds,
    Stormy winds that do his bidding,

You mountains and all hills,	Solo
Fruit trees and all cedars,	Solo
Wild animals and all cattle,	Solo
Small creatures and flying birds,	Solo
Kings of the earth and all nations,	All
You princes and all rulers on earth,	
Young men and maidens,	Girls
Old men and children,	Boys
Let them praise the name of the Lord,	Girls
For his name alone is exalted;	Boys
His splendor is above the earth and the heavens.	All

Praise the Lord!

Sentence Starters:

"If Jesus had not been born, . . ."

"If Easter had not happened, . . ."

"When I read the Bible, . . ."

"When I hear the word *faith* I think of. . . ."

To stimulate children's thinking, put an unfinished sentence on the chalkboard. Ask students to think about possible conclusions and write them down, or simply ask them to respond orally. They may write only one sentence or conclude the sentence in several different ways or use it as the beginning of a paragraph. To make Sentence Starters a more creative activity, begin the sentences this way: "The Bible is like a. . ."; "Faith is. . ."; "Trusting is. . . ." Older children sometimes develop interesting similies and metaphors for familiar truths.

Read the sentences aloud and compare children's ideas. Discuss other ideas that may emerge, checking them with Scripture when appropriate. Be positive about all contributions and gentle in correcting misinterpretations. Consolidate the sentences for a special reading to include in the worship time, perhaps illustrated with art work.

The activities discussed in this chapter are representative of many more which can be used in children's church. Still others can be devised by creative and prayerful teachers. A chart of good activities is included on page 175. Directions for most of them can be found in the books listed in the Appendix.

Notes

1. David P. Ausabel, "The Transition from Concrete to Abstract Cognitive Functioning," *The Journal of Research in Science Teaching*, vol. 2, issue 3, 1964, p. 261.
2. This activity is included in *Growing in God's Family Guidebook for Church Time*, Gospel Light Publications, p. 75.
3. Kamir Olson, "I'm Four—I'm Learning about God," *The Alliance Teacher*, summer issue, 1979, p. 3.
4. Craig Pearson, "Can You Keep Quiet for Three Seconds?" *Learning*, February issue, 1980, p. 41.

7

Time for Worship

To worship is—
 to quicken the conscience by the holiness of God,
 to feed the mind with the truth of God
 to purge the imagination by the beauty of God
 to open the heart to the love of God
 to devote the will to the purpose of God.[1]

E. M. Baxter

Preparing the Environment

Jesus taught anywhere. He taught in the streets, in private homes, on the highway, at a village well, from a boat on the lake. He taught at the drop of an opportunity: a question from a friend, a challenge from an enemy, the sight of a bare fig tree, or a widow's quiet sacrifice. Any of these was enough to spark an unforgettable lesson. Reading through the gospels one gets the impression that most of Jesus' teaching took place in the crucible of life's unplanned contingencies, and surely some of our most meaningful lessons are learned that way. Nevertheless, on certain occasions, and especially when a particular revelation of Himself was involved, Jesus carefully planned and structured the learning experience.

We see in John chapter 7 that when Jesus went up to Jerusalem for the feast of tabernacles, He deliberately timed His arrival for the middle of the week when curiosity about Him was at its peak and speculation pro and con was rampant in temple and marketplace. He went directly to the center of activity, to the porch of the temple, and there engaged friend and foe alike in a presentation of His deity and mission. On the last and greatest day of the feast, He chose the climax of the ceremony to call all men to faith. Edersheim says of this moment that as water gushed forth from the golden pitcher, in the silence that followed that symbolic act, "There arose, so loud as to be heard throughout the Temple, the voice of Jesus: '*If any man thirst, let him come unto Me and drink!*' "[2] Jesus seemed to time His invitation to come at the high point of the feast.

At the Transfiguration, also, we see Jesus arranging an environment that would dramatize and heighten the impact of His listeners' experience.[3] Alone on Mount Hermon He led Peter, James, and John to an awesome confrontation with His deity. They were overwhelmed by His splendor and authority as a succession of astonishing events took place: Jesus' garments glistened an unearthly white, Moses and Elijah appeared, a cloud descended, and God spoke audibly of His Son. Decades later, in their writings, John would refer to Christ's deity as "that which we have seen and heard," and Peter would recall that soul-sundering experience with Jesus on the holy mount.

On the evening before His death, in preparation for a long and very personal discourse with His disciples, Jesus carefully orchestrated the environment and sequence of events (Luke 22:10-13). From His initial and very precise directions concerning *which* house and *which* room, through the instructive washing of the disciples' feet, the symbolic sharing of the bread and wine, and the final singing of a hymn, Jesus led the disciples to intimate fellowship and reverent worship.

Like learning, worship can be a spontaneous and unplanned experience. More often it is aroused by ideas, events, and impressions that overwhelm and inspire. This kind of worship should be carefully planned, prayed for, and protected. For those of us who lead children's church, it represents our highest privilege and most demanding task.

The Worship Leader

So much depends on the leader in worship! What is this person's attitude toward the children's church hour? Does he or she see it as further opportunity for instruction, or as having a different purpose altogether? How does the teacher perceive the children who make up the "congregation?" Does he or she believe they are really capable of worship?

Does the leader have a deep personal *awareness of God's presence?* Is he or she one who has known the joys of worship in the closet and the sanctuary? To a great extent, the children's experience of worship will depend upon the leader's own sense of the Holy. Leaders need to cultivate in their devotional lives a sensitivity to the power and presence of God, that "high and lofty One who inhabiteth eternity, whose name is Holy" (Isa. 57:15).

As leaders we must *know the capacities and abilities of the children we lead*—the factors of family and school life which influence them, the levels of intelligence and development which challenge or limit, the measure of their spiritual awareness and need. This knowledge cannot all come from books and training courses, as helpful as these are. Some must come from observation. Leaders should endeavor to learn about individual children, observing them carefully in church and outside and keeping notes on their progress.

Early in the year teachers will have to be patient with themselves and the learners as both get to know each other. However, as the year progresses, they will find themselves able to lead children to worship with greater wisdom and effectiveness. Leaders must avoid choosing the same responsive children over and over, but attempt instead to help those who may seem less capable to contribute at their highest possible level. Vocal, verbal, Stephen might be happy to read Scripture every Sunday, but teachers should work as well with underachiever Michael until he feels comfortable reading a carefully prepared passage in his turn.

The leader also must *know the curriculum*—not only today's program but what has come before and what lies ahead. He or she must know what resources are available and how they can be secured.

In preparing for worship the leader *must be thorough.* Particularly for the worship service itself, one must plan, review, and rehearse (at least mentally) until one feels sure of content and procedure. Fellow workers should not be forgotten; they must also have a copy of the order of service.

Timing is another factor the leader must consider. When planning the length of the service and when conducting it, discipline yourself by the clock. But do not be rigid about it! Only if interest and participation are very high should the time be extended, and then not for long. Better to end *before* worship has become tiring.

To out-flank fatigue, that ever-present threat to the second hour program, plan worship no later than the middle of the hour—for young children even earlier. With older ones, if twelve o'clock arrives and the adult service continues, do not extend the children's service beyond its proper length. Do not dismiss the children, either! Conclude as planned, then have games, books, records, and tapes available for children to use until their parents arrive.

The leader's manner will set the pace for children's worship. If leaders are quiet, reverent, and joyous, most of the children will be, too. Conduct the service in a friendly, natural style, but maintain the dignity a worship service requires. Read and speak clearly, distinctly, and with feeling. Practice what Baxter calls "an economy of words,"[4] avoiding any comments or actions which would interfere with the even flow of the service. If you have to discipline, do it unobtrusively. A long, meaningful look is often enough to curb misbehavior; if not, correct with a whisper in the ear or a gentle hand on the shoulder. Rather than spoiling the spirit of the service by scolding, signal to another teacher to remove a disruptive child. The teacher should stay with the child until he is able to return to the group. Throughout the service, whether leading music, praying, or speaking, leaders can reflect an attitude of joy in the task, knowing that they worship even as they serve.

The Worship Atmosphere

After the leader himself, the atmosphere of the church room may be the most important factor to affect the children's worship. Children are very sensitive to the atmosphere of a place. They cannot get beyond it, as adults can, and function in spite of negative conditions. If the room is dark and cluttered, if furniture and air temperature are uncomfortable, if there are visual distractions (noise seems less of a factor), or overcrowding, children's worship will be impeded.

The first responsibility of the leader, then, is to provide an atmosphere conducive to worship. The area chosen for assembly will be important. If possible, take the children to an adjoining room in the department. Chairs and a worship center can then be set up ahead of time and left undisturbed. If a separate room is not available, designate one part of your room as the worship area. One church very effectively made one end of a long room the focus of worship by installing a ceiling spotlight. At the proper time the rest of the room was darkened and the worship area was flooded with a soft light.

The worship center should be set up near the front of

the group. Make it simple: a table with an open Bible, a small vase of fresh flowers, and a picture is enough. Sometimes replace the flowers with other objects of natural beauty—a flowering plant, a beautiful shell or rock formation. Choose pictures carefully and change them often. For preschool departments, a painting of Jesus with a group of children might be used; for older groups, use one of Frances Hook's portraits of Christ or other paintings that are well done and not so familiar that they will go unnoticed. Some teachers place the worship table in front of a bulletin board or screen where mounted pictures can be changed with the season or the unit theme.

The children's own art work as well as professional pictures should be displayed. Paintings might be displayed temporarily; banners and stained-glass designs could be part of a more permanent background. One class needed a portable backdrop for a worship center which had to be removed each Sunday. The teacher cut three large, gothic-shaped panels from dark blue poster board. The children cut designs and shapes out of bright construction paper and pasted them, stained-glass style, on the poster board. The panels were then hinged with masking tape, so the "window" could stand independently and be folded up for storage each week.

Chairs should face the worship center, but also allow children to see each other. A single or double-row semicircle works well. Space the chairs so that elbows do not bump, and the rows far enough apart to discourage playful footwork. Children will see better that way, too. Chairs will inevitably be inched closer and that is seldom worth fussing over, but avoid starting out with a problem by overcrowding the seating arrangement. Teachers should sit with the children, not off to one side or in the back of the room. They are participants, not observers.

The Call to Worship

The way the service begins will help or hinder the atmosphere for worship. Several minutes ahead of time give a clearly understood signal that it is time to clean up and prepare for worship. Flicker the lights, play a chord on the piano, or start a clean-up song. Speak softly now; as teachers drop their voices children will sense a change of purpose. After a few minutes begin a piano prelude or have a guitarist strum a favorite song as children gather. Preschoolers respond to a "walk to church" led by a teacher or to a child's ringing a Melode' Bell. Teach children to enter quietly, as they would into the church sanctuary. They should feel that they are not *playing* church but are a *part* of the church, gathering for worship.

Early in the year talk about these procedures in the small groups. If you establish desirable behaviors early in the church year, children are likely to continue them. If, instead, they learn patterns of confusion and disorder, better habits will be difficult—though not impossible—to establish.

An adult, usually the lead teacher, should give the Call to Worship. The leader's manner, tone of voice, and warmth of expression will be reflected in the group. Stand front and center (remain seated with preschoolers) and wait for full attention. Children should learn early that talking or inattention are not acceptable when the Bible is read. Read a call to worship like Psalm 67:5, "Let the people praise thee, O God; let all the people praise thee." After a few weeks, you may want children to respond aloud after you read the first part of the verse. Move immediately to the next part of the service, preferably one that involves everyone like singing a hymn or the Doxology. Avoid irrelevant comments about children's bright happy faces or how they should sit up straight. If you think they need help with a proper posture for worship discuss it during small group time. Later a smile and simple straightening of your shoulders will cue them in.

The Worshipers

Before going any further we should take a look at the worshipers themselves to consider how the differences in their development will affect the structure of the worship service. We have already pointed out that the younger the child, the shorter and less formal should be the program. Let us review the worship capabilities of each two-year age span.

Twos and Threes worship *spontaneously,* in response to the wonders they discover in the unfolding of their daily lives. The teacher prayerfully anticipates opportunities to help individual children praise God for the wonderful things He has done. She or he knows such opportunities come at unexpected times and cannot always be planned for. Gathering for corporate worship should be very brief—singing, prayer, and a simple story will be sufficient. Teachers should sit or kneel with children on the floor or sit in small chairs.

Fours and Fives can be led in an *informal* worship time, centering on songs of praise, stories with a scriptural theme, and conversational prayer. Plan about a ten-minute service for fours and about fifteen minutes for fives. Begin the year with less time, and work up to the maximum as children mature. You will see noticeable differences in their abilities in the course of one year.

Because the time for worship is so short, make every minute count. More of your planning and prayer should go into that ten- or fifteen-minute service than into any other segment of the morning's program. Remember that for all preschoolers, including kindergarteners, the basic approach is still that of "seizing spontaneous opportunities and using them to share moments of beauty, wonder, or compassion."[5]

Young children's worship should sometimes take place outside in God's world. There is no better environment for praise than a quiet, grassy spot under a sheltering tree.

Sixes and Sevens are ready for a *loosely structured* program of worship. Plan for them to become increasingly involved as the year progresses and their language skills improve. Second graders can help younger ones find Scripture passages and the pages in the children's hymnal. Follow a simple order of service in which they can participate. You might even print it on the chalkboard or on a permanent chart.

Call to Worship	Psalm 150:1,2,6
Hymn #29	"To God Be the Glory"
Scripture Reading	Luke 15:11-19
Offering	Doxology
Message by Grade Two	The Story of the Runaway Son (Slide Presentation)
Prayer	
Song	"I Have Decided to Follow Jesus"

Eights and Nines are at an ideal age for *training* in worship. They can prepare and contribute any number of items and activities to enrich the worship service. For middlers, follow the order of service above, perhaps adding a Benediction or Response, and developing each element more fully. The service now can extend to about thirty minutes. On some Sundays include a choir number, choral reading or other special feature prepared by a small group. Some leaders have children this age participate as ushers or assistants in their worship program. They lead children in, bring the offering forward for dedication, announce hymns and assist in other ways. It is possible to stress their responsibility by having them sit on chairs placed at each side of the worship center. Before the message, they join the congregation. Of course, the privilege of being an assistant should rotate among children.

While all these activities are meant to foster participation and a reverent attitude, guard against imposing an unnatural formality. Eight- and nine-year-olds are, after all, children—casual, uninhibited, and spontaneous. Be relaxed and friendly at worship as at other times. We can take our example from Jesus, who accepted children as they were. He never tried to make little adults out of them.

Tens and Elevens, by and large, are ready to *participate in the adult service* part of the time or even regularly. If they have experienced a good children's worship program, they understand and can respond to the prayers, hymns, and Scripture readings in the sanctuary. Physically and intellectually, most fifth and sixth graders can meet the demands of an hour of inactivity and focused attention. Also, there is value in children's worshiping with their parents for a couple years before returning to the peer-group stratification of junior and senior high when the family pew almost universally yields to the youth-group pew. For these reasons, most churches encourage juniors to join in the adult service.

Churches which decide to provide a separate worship service for juniors have several options. (1) Juniors can use the entire hour for training in worship, developing their own programs with adult guidance. Doctrine, church history, missions, and sacred music can be stressed during these years. (2) They can sit through the first part of the service and be dismissed before the sermon to walk quietly to a location where a message will be geared to their level. (3) Some churches have an on-again, off-again schedule where older children stay in the sanctuary for the pastor's message one Sunday, then leave early the next Sunday to discuss it. A work sheet with an outline and questions is provided for the Sunday they hear the message. Of course, this requires close cooperation between pastor and church time leaders. This method effectively trains youngsters to listen and respond mentally to the message—an invaluable habit to carry into adolescence and adulthood.

Churches that drop the church time program at age ten can use sermon work sheets every week for youngsters in the sanctuary. These pose questions and solicit reactions to certain parts of the sermon. They are collected and read by a Sunday school teacher or the pastor. Each one is returned with positive comments or at least a thank you. The pastor reinforces the use of the work sheets by referring to them occasionally in his message. Some adults have been known to sneak a copy of the work sheets for their own edification!

Notes

1. Edna M. Baxter, *Learning to Worship* (Valley Forge: Judson, 1965), p. 19.
2. Alfred Edersheim, *Jesus the Messiah* (Grand Rapids: Wm. B. Eerdmans Publishing Co., 1954), p. 319.
3. James Michael Lee discusses Jesus' structuring of the Transfiguration environment in *The Shape of Religious Instruction* (Dayton: Pflaum, 1971).
4. Baxter, *Learning to Worship*, p. 76.
5. Marvin Taylor, *An Introduction to Christian Education* (Nashville: Abingdon Press, 1966), p. 246.

8

The Elements of Worship

Check your church bulletin on any month of Sundays. More than likely the order of service will include the same items from week to week, usually in the same order. Christians of every persuasion seem to feel that prayer, Scripture reading, singing, and preaching are essential elements in worship. Usually, the elements center around a biblical theme or a season of the church year. In children's worship the same elements and unity of theme should be present, even though the length of the service may vary from a few minutes to half an hour.

Music in Worship

It is difficult to conceive of worship without music. Music is an avenue to the emotions, a channel of expression, a persuader of the will. When in the best of the church's hymns, fine music is wedded to moving language, the effect on the worshiper is profound. A. W. Tozer advised Christians to prime the devotional pump by including a hymnbook as well as a Bible in their private worship.

From the earliest days of their allegiance to Jehovah, the Hebrews sang their worship. Deborah and Barak sang praise for God's deliverance (Judg. 5:3). David and Solomon held the ministry of music on the level of prophecy. The Chronicler spoke of the master musician Jeduthun as one who "prophesied with a harp" and he expected the temple musicians to "prophesy with harps, with psalteries, and with cymbals" (1 Chron. 25:1-3). Levites were appointed in large numbers as cantors in temple worship. From the tribe of Levi 288 musicians, trained to sing in the temple, "junior and senior, master and pupil alike" took turns in their duties at worship.

In the New Testament Jesus sang with His disciples, and Paul quoted the words of well-known early church hymns. Colossians 3:16 admonishes Christians to "encourage one another in psalms and hymns and spiritual songs," indicating that music was an important element in first-century gatherings of the church.

Music should play a large part in any children's worship program. To inspire a reverent mood, play a hymn softly on the piano or organ or use an instrumental recording as children enter. After the call to worship, have children respond by singing softly the familiar "Halleluiah" or "God Is So Good." Older children who play instruments can contribute to worship if they are reasonably well skilled for their age. Young children can be taught to play a simple prelude on the Melode' Bells or an autoharp or xylophone.

In each service use carefully selected hymns of the church as well as children's songs and choruses. Use only those that include concrete and understandable language. As children mature, they should come to know and love some of the sacred music of Bach, Wesley, Luther, Simpson, Crosby, Watts, and other great singers of Christian life and doctrine.

Illustrate a new hymn with glossy magazine pictures or fine art. Show the pictures as words are displayed. This will help children focus on the ideas in the song as well as on the rhythm and melody. Try not to teach new songs during worship. Instead, play a recording of the song ahead of time, let a small group learn it and sing it as a choir, and then have the whole group sing it the next Sunday.

Children will feel more comfortable with the song and will participate better. In this way the hymnody of the young congregation will continually grow.

How to Select Songs

Worship leaders will want to begin immediately collecting a wide variety of appropriate songs. Books with good selections are listed in the Appendix. Your own church hymnal should also provide many selections. The following are questions to keep in mind as you choose songs for children.

1. *Is the song worshipful?* There may be some place in the child's experience for action choruses like "Climb, Climb, up Sunshine Mountain," or "Deep and Wide," but it is definitely not in the children's church service! Nothing about these songs helps the singer focus on God or express love for Him. Every musical selection should serve the purpose of worship.
2. *Are the concepts concrete, and is the vocabulary on the children's level?* I was surprised one morning to walk into a middler worship service and find the children singing the chorus, "His Banner over Me Is Love." The words and images from Song of Solomon were meaningful to the leaders—that is why they chose the song—but the concepts were lost on the children. They responded well because they liked the melody and the guitar accompaniment, but they could not share the symbolic meanings of the words. St. Paul's advice to the Corinthians to sing praises "not only with the spirit but with the mind as well," (1 Cor. 14:15) instructs us also in our choice of songs. Choose those with

words that can be understood literally, like "All Things Bright and Beautiful" or "Praise Him."[1] An occasional word beyond the child's vocabulary level is acceptable—that gives him something to reach for—but too many such words tempt children to put their brains on "hold" until the song is over or, worse, to make up their own meanings for inexplicable terms. One child who grew up in the church was surprised to learn at about age ten the real words to "Lead On, O King Eternal." He had always heard and sung it as "Lead On, O Kingly Turtle," and rather enjoyed the odd mental image that aroused (which confirms our suspicion that children do not really *expect* church songs to make sense!).

3. *Are the length, rhythm, and range of the song suited to the children's development?* Children should enjoy the music they sing! They will not enjoy it if the tune is difficult or not melodious. Young children need brief, two- or three-line songs with simple rhythm and melody, preferably ranging within the octave above middle C. Older children can handle a wider range and more complex rhythm, but avoid extreme leaps in the melody or songs with a difficult tempo. Excellent song books for children are readily available and can provide leaders with a wealth of inspiring music for children. Some are listed in the Appendix.

How to Teach Songs

Preschoolers must learn their music by ear—a good way for anyone to learn songs! A teacher with a good singing voice (not necessarily solo quality—just pleasant and on key) is probably the best instrument for teaching at this age. A piano sometimes overwhelms young voices so play it softly, or use instead an autoharp, zither, or guitar, stressing the melody. Sing the song through for the children, perhaps illustrating it with pictures. Then ask them to try to move their lips to say the words as you sing. Next, sing it and let them supply a phrase here and there or sing the refrain. Finally, have them sing the entire song.

Primary children, too, should hear the song sung through or played instrumentally before attempting to learn it. Write the words on chart paper or tagboard mounted at the front of the room. This will help them lift their heads and project their voices. Using color and illustrations on the chart will clarify and add interest. Have teachers learn the songs ahead of time to lend support to the children's voices. Give them a tape recording to help them learn it, if necessary.

Occasionally, ask your learners questions to be sure they understand the key words and concepts in a hymn. If, however, you find yourself having to do this often, you had better consider whether the song is too advanced for your children. Too much explaining takes the joy out of singing!

Middlers and juniors should use a hymnbook as much as possible. Help the uninitiated learn the special way hymns are read, not line by line, but verse by verse. Ask your church music committee for slightly worn copies of your church hymnal to use in children's church. You need only one for each pair of children—it is good for them to learn to share a hymnal. Plan a project for the children to put their own creative covers on the books, and add a supplement of children's songs in the back.

Older children should become as familiar as possible with hymns they will sing all their lives. With some of the more difficult ones, consider learning only as much of the hymn as the children can appreciate and sing well. For example, "Praise to the Lord, the Almighty," can be shortened by half without doing violence to the words. The children can enjoy the first part of the hymn and avoid the wide leaps in melody that make the latter half more difficult. Later, when the hymn sounds forth from the sanctuary organ, it will seem like an old friend.

The 1978 edition of *Hymns of the Christian Life*[2] includes many selections which school-age children can learn in whole or in part. Here is a list of hymns, choruses, and responses from which to choose. Those which can be sung by preschoolers as well are marked with an asterisk.

Worship and Adoration	Page
*Alleluia	605
Come, Thou Almighty King	3
Day Is Dying in the West (Chorus)	571
Fairest Lord Jesus	48
Holy, Holy	600
Holy, Holy, Holy, Lord God Almighty	2
How Great Thou Art	33
Joyful, Joyful, We Adore Thee	16
Oh for a Thousand Tongues	44
The Lord Is in His Holy Temple	595
This Is My Father's World	28

Praise

All Creatures of Our God and King	24
All People That on Earth Do Dwell	20
For the Beauty of the Earth	26
*God Is So Good	607
He Is Lord	596
Praise to the Lord, the Almighty	10
Praise the Savior, Ye Who Know Him	45

To God Be the Glory	29
What a Wonderful Savior	527

Prayer

Eternal Father, Strong to Save	9
May the Mind of Christ, My Savior	257
Savior, Like a Shepherd, Lead Us	344

A. B. Simpson's Hymns

Yesterday, Today, Forever (Chorus)	119
Step by Step (*Chorus)	349
Thy Kingdom Come	472

The Church Year

Hosanna, Loud Hosanna	80
Christ the Lord Is Risen Today	99
Come Ye Thankful People Come	573
We Gather Together	572

(All Christmas carols are loved; the following are especially suited to children.)

Joy to the World!	52
*Away in a Manger	54
Once in Royal David's City	55
While Shepherds Watched Their Flocks by Night	60
Oh Come, All Ye Faithful (*Chorus)	68
What Child Is This, Who Laid to Rest?	72

Prayer as Worship

It was the Sunday after Thanksgiving. Our middler children had learned all month about giving praise to God. We had sung, painted, role played, and talked about reasons to praise Him. Now, with the Thanksgiving celebration behind us and Christmas ahead, we focused on prayer in the worship time. After Scripture and a brief message on prayer, the leader asked the children to say a personal "Thank you" to God. Each of us would write a short note to God thanking Him for one thing He had done for us or had given to us which we especially appreciated that day. Then we passed out small white stationery notes with "Thank You" written in gold letters on the front. Inside each child would write a prayer of thanks. The teacher would read the notes aloud, but not names. ("God knows our handwriting anyway," one child observed.) Heads bent and shoulders hunched as children wrote intently. Then all bowed in prayer as the teacher read each thank you note aloud. One child thanked God for the good family meal they had had on Thursday. A girl who had lost her mother a few months before thanked Him for "my Daddy, who works every day and takes care of us." A small fourth grader expressed thanks for his "athletic ability." Every child shared in prayer that morning, and we sensed a spirit of worship together.

Children need to experience prayer as talking to God. They perceive it too often as a way of performing in front of a group or a means of pleasing adults. In the privacy of their hearts children *do* pray, and they will be more likely to pray during worship if we encourage them gently and if we model prayer that is sincere and personal communication with God.

Teacher-led Prayer

Adults should not dominate opportunities for prayer in the worship service. However, it is important that they provide a pattern for children to follow as they begin to pray aloud. Christian educator Paul Vieth says that leading a group in prayer is the most difficult part of conducting worship. He counsels the leading adults to avoid hackneyed words and pious phrases in their prayers. "Bless Your Word as it's given forth" and "Grant them journeying mercies" are examples of overworked lines that seem to be heard only in public prayer, never in "real life." Prayer is addressed to God, Vieth reminds us, "It is not an occasion for moral admonitions addressed to the congregation."[3] ("Help us to sit still and listen well this morning, Lord.") The prayer leader's voice should be natural and sincere, with no trace of sanctimoniousness.

Vieth further suggests that the content of any prayer should include one or more of the five elements of prayer—adoration, confession, thanksgiving, supplication, submission—remembered by some as the ACTSS of prayer. Be brief, be simple, be concrete. It is a good idea to write out your prayer ahead of time though you will want to speak it, not read it, in the service. Study the prayers of Scripture, both Old and New Testament, to enrich the concepts and vocabulary of your prayers. Ephesians 3:14-21 records Paul's fervent expression of adoration and supplication, assurance and hope, as he bows his knees unto the Father on behalf of his brothers in Ephesus. Jesus' prayers in the gospels and David's in the psalms can teach us the language of prayer and its spirit.

Help children to understand that when one person leads, he is expressing the prayers of the whole group. This will become clear as you solicit children's contributions to prayer, perhaps listing on the chalkboard their concerns, with names of people or situations that need prayer as well as expressions of thanks to God for specific acts of love and grace. They will learn that in crisis situations the Christian's first response is to bring the situation to God. Like us, children are quicker to remember needs than to return thanks. Leaders can help them learn the response of praise by following up requests and mentioning answered prayer.

Silent Prayer

In our noisy world, a moment of silence seems a rare gift. Even in worship we are often surrounded by voices, instruments, scraping feet, outside traffic. Help children cultivate the ability to "Be still, and know that I am God." Instead of praying aloud some mornings, suggest ideas for prayer and ask children to talk to God in their own minds or just to think about Him for a quiet moment. Mary LeBar suggests that the leader show pictures from the story or of lovely created things as the children meditate. A verse of Scripture written on a poster can also create a focus for silent prayer.[4] Take advantage of moments when the children grow quiet, responding to a moving song or story. Suggest that they speak silently to God about whatever they are thinking. Then give them time—as long as possible —and close with a simple "Amen."

Children's Prayers

I am not sure Paul Vieth is right about the worship leaders' most difficult task. An even greater challenge than leading in prayer is helping children learn to do it. Not that children cannot learn *prayers*—memorizing a prayer is an easy skill to teach and acquire. Once a child has the words of a prayer mastered, he can recite it almost any time. But few of us are satisfied for our children to know only that kind of praying. We believe prayer should usually be spontaneous, like conversation. So we encourage children to offer prayer in the group, hoping all will participate but usually finding that the same few repeatedly volunteer. Even children from Christian homes may suffer an attack of shyness when asked to pray aloud. Like being sent to the chalkboard to do long division, praying in public seems to shut down the brain.

The key to teaching children to pray in public is to help them feel comfortable about it. Start as early as possible—at age two, or whenever they can talk—and continue each year helping them to pray aloud. Never insist; merely support. To a soft-spoken child say, "We wanted to pray with you, but couldn't hear all your words. Would you pray them a little louder?" To a reluctant one, "Maybe you could help us pray today. Let's think what you could say to God."

Take the pressure off the individual by having everyone read a prayer together. That will help novices get used to the sound of their own voice in prayer. With young children say a few words to God and have them repeat after you; with older ones, put a Scripture verse on the board and pray it aloud together.

Sometimes ask everyone in the circle to say a sentence prayer. Few children will refuse to join in when everyone else is praying. At first, suggest that everyone start with the same words, like, "Lord Jesus, I'm glad today for _____ _____." Children can finish the prayer by naming a person, thing, or experience for which they are grateful. Later, this pattern may help them form their own sentence prayers.

Primaries and older children sometimes like to pray in pairs, sharing their requests, needs, and items of praise and then praying together about them. Teachers may want to pair up with children who are reluctant or unpredictable but should be ready for surprises—some of the least cooperative children will take this kind of praying seriously.

Formal Prayers

One way of having children participate in prayer is to teach them to say "Amen" at the end of formal prayer. The youngest child can learn this simple response and is more likely to realize as he matures that the leader prays not only for himself, but for all those gathered in worship. Sung responses like those mentioned in the music section are a good way for children to pray audibly. The Doxology and the Gloria Patri are formal prayer responses primaries can learn. Older children should study the Lord's Prayer as part of the worship curriculum, focusing first on the meanings and pattern of the prayer and later committing it to memory. Many congregations repeat the Lord's Prayer in the worship service. Children of eight or nine should be prepared to join in this act of devotion.

Guard against prayer's becoming routine, a slot to be filled in the order of service. Be as creative planning prayer as in other activities. In all worship experiences, let prayers be joyful, short, and to the point. Let them be sung, spoken, silent, and shared; let them be offered by children as well as by adults. Let prayer become a natural communication with the God who is with us, nearer than breathing, closer than hands or feet.

Offering

Since our gifts and tithes to God are aspects of worship, offering should not be neglected in the children's worship service even though it sometimes presents special problems.

Most children are in Sunday school the first hour, and their natural inclination is to drop all their offerings in the

Sunday school basket—probably a good idea, considering how often money is lost or played with during the morning. That means few children have any offering remaining for children's church. It seems defeating to pass an empty basket around week after week for only an occasional teacher or child to use. One solution is to ask the Sunday school leaders to let the offering remain in the basket through the children's church hour, counting it only after additional contributions have been collected. Another idea is to have a closed container, decorated attractively, into which offering can be dropped as soon as children arrive. Then at the right time in the service, a child carries the offering receptacle forward to be dedicated in prayer.

When discussing offering with the children, perhaps during a unit on worship, try to develop foundational concepts of stewardship. Teach that Christians are responsible to use part of the money God provides them with to see that everyone hears the gospel—people in our community and those far away in every part of the world. Children should understand too, that the church uses some of the offering money to buy things the congregation needs for worship and teaching—furniture, hymnbooks, fuel, crayons, and Sunday school papers. Avoid vague generalities about giving our money to Jesus (they see us give it to a lady down the hall) or for "the Lord's work." Elsiebeth McDaniels, editor at Scripture Press, tells how a primary child responded when she asked him to explain why we give some of our money to God: "Well, He did all that work, didn't He?" To that boy, our offerings were God's wages!

When prayer is made for the offering, let it be a simple sentence, "We're glad to bring our love gifts, Father, to help keep your church warm and bright." Or, "to help send Bibles to the children of Ivory Coast."

Scripture in Worship

It is early autumn in Jerusalem; the year, 457 B.C. In the square of the city a large crowd gathers around Ezra the Scribe, official delegate of the royal court of Artexerxes, and a leader of the returning exiles. Ezra holds in his hand a rare treasure—a scroll of the books of Moses. Written in Hebrew, the now seldom-spoken language of God's people, the Law of the Lord has not been heard in Judah in anyone's memory. As the ancient words sound across the square and are interpreted, the listeners kneel and weep. So broken are they by the power of the spoken Word that Ezra must reassure them, "This day is holy unto our Lord; neither be ye sorry: for the joy of the Lord is your strength" (Neh. 8:10).

We can learn from this passage a great deal about eliciting good attitudes and response when God's Word is read in worship. First, the preceding verses tell us that the word was read to *those who could understand* it, and the listeners *were attentive* (v. 3). Ezra stood in a prominent place where he could be seen by all (v. 5), and when he opened the scroll, *all the people stood up,* Ezra blessed the Lord, and *the people responded to his words,* "Amen, Amen." As Ezra read, teachers *caused the people to understand* (v. 7) and *gave the sense* (v. 8). Those who heard were moved emotionally: *they wept* (v. 9) and they also rejoiced: "All the people went their way to eat, and to drink, and to send portions and to make great mirth," (v. 12) because they understood the message of God's love. Finally, the last half of the chapter tells how the people *obeyed* the commands they heard in the law, and kept a solemn assembly.

How can this chapter help us be better leaders of worship? Notice that the reading of the Scripture puts responsibility on both leader and listener: the leader to arrange the best conditions for learning, the listener to respond in a manner worthy of God's message. We can derive these practical principles from chapter 8 of Nehemiah:

1. Read those portions of Scripture your children can understand.
2. Read Scripture clearly, expressively, and with authority.
3. Read only when the Word has the children's full attention. Expect this no matter who is reading the Bible aloud.
4. Welcome an expression of emotion in response to the Word, from yourself as well as from the children. Smiling, singing, (even clapping hands!) bowing in prayer, and offering private or public commitment are all appropriate reactions to hearing God's message.
5. Teach a consistent response to the Scripture—a sung or spoken "Amen," a choral response, or a silent meditation.
6. Aim for an outcome of obedience as the meaning of the Word is brought to bear on children's lives.

Use an open Bible whenever Scripture is read, even if it is only one verse or if the passage is written on a chart. Do not dilute the impact of a Bible passage by reading it from a lesson book. Little children can participate by finding the passage in your Bible if you put a colored marker in the proper place. Let older groups read a passage aloud together, or prepare one or two children ahead of time to read the Scripture of the morning.

Some teachers find it a problem that young readers bring a variety of translations to church. If your church has one version of the Scripture it prefers, ask that Bibles in that version be supplied for the program. If not, turn the problem to an advantage by reading different versions of key verses. Say "Eric, let us hear the verse in your translation, and then we'll hear it in yours, Monica." Children will soon learn that there are different ways to state the same truth. By comparing translations, they will gain insight into the meanings of the original words and begin to understand why we have many versions of the Bible.

Responsive Reading

Primary children can learn to read responsively if you start with a litany like Psalm 136:1-9. The leader could read the first part of the verse and have the children respond with the refrain, "For His lovingkindness is everlasting." Later, as middlers or juniors, children should learn to read responsively from the Scripture selections in the hymnal.

Keep the reading of Scripture fresh and vital by varying the method with choral readings, art work, and other means. I once observed an especially meaningful rendering of Psalm 147 illustrated with slides. A primary teacher had taken slides of her vacation trip to northern Canada. During worship a child read the verses as selected slides were flashed on the wall. Scenes from the Canadian wilderness captured the beauty of the psalmist's word-pictures: "Who covers the heavens with clouds, Who provides rain for the earth, Who makes grass to grow on the mountains ...He gives snow like wool;...He casts forth His ice as fragments;...He causes His wind to blow and the waters to flow .... Praise the Lord!" (NASB)[5]

The Worship Message

"Perhaps the most common pitfall for the leader of children," says Mary LeBar, "is the temptation to teach, rather than to lead to worship; to tell, rather than to elicit a response toward God."[6]

It is natural for us to teach—there is so much we want children to know! We instinctively look for opportunities to review, to remind, to drill, to instruct our children in Bible facts and Scripture memorization. Too often these activities, good in themselves, have displaced the worship emphasis in children's church. The worship leader has a goal beyond instruction. She must ask, "Will this message I am preparing lead the children to worship and adore God? Will it elicit a response of obedience and faith?" The worship message must do more than teach; it must appeal to the emotions and to the will as well as to the mind.

We need to ponder the significance of the New Testament distinction between *teaching* and *preaching. To teach* in the original Greek is *matheteuo* (to disciple) or *didasko* (to hold discourse in order to instruct). These words imply an interactive process like that which takes place in small groups. *To preach,* on the other hand, is *kerusso* (to herald, or *proclaim,* as a messenger would announce the words of the king).[7] Our purpose in the worship message is to *proclaim* God's Word in a way that will inspire and encourage the hearers to respond to God. Both the *content* and the *method* of a proclamation receive a different emphasis than they might in a teaching situation. Let us consider both of these aspects of the message.

The Content of the Message

We have mentioned before the importance of correlating church time and Sunday school themes so that a unified curriculum is experienced by regularly attending children. If the publisher of your church hour curriculum is the same as the one you use for Sunday school, content should be expected to mesh well and worship aims should be clear. Many churches, however, use a variety of materials for children's church, or simply expand on the

Sunday school material. In such cases special efforts should be made to develop worship aims and to see that a good balance of worship content is achieved. The following are important themes for the church-time program to develop.

1. *The nature of Christian worship.* What does it mean to worship God? How do we worship? Why have we come to worship in this way? These are questions the church-time program should consider. From their first years in the church children should learn the ways we worship God in prayer, song, stewardship, and witness. As they mature, children should increase their awareness of Christian hymnology, early church practices, and the meanings behind our present order of service. Old Testament passages on the tabernacle and temple, and selections from Acts and the epistles will provide rich material on the roots of our worship practices.

    Once or twice a year take school-age children to the sanctuary to observe parts of the adult service. Tell them ahead of time what to watch for—the physical appointments of the sanctuary, the people who offer their talents to God—pianists, organists, choir members, ushers, preacher—and the attitudes of worshipers. Studying the church family—pastor, elders, deacons, teachers, helpers—leads to appreciation for God's love and provision in establishing the church as a spiritual body.

    Study a church bulletin and discuss together the meaning of each element on the program. Older children can learn to plan their own order of service and use it one Sunday. The children's worship service will begin to have greater meaning for them as they understand the history and significance of the Christian assembly.

2. *Doctrines.* Reading through Paul's epistles, one is impressed with how often Paul's explanations of doctrinal truth inspired lyrical outbursts of praise. Try as he would to be didactic and practical, the glory kept breaking through! Describing the reality of the indwelling Christ to Ephesian Christians, he concluded by exulting, "To Him be the glory in the church and in Christ Jesus to all generations forever and ever. Amen" (Eph. 3:21, NASB). Giving pastoral advice to Timothy, he broke into an early hymn extolling "the King of kings and Lord of lords" (1 Tim. 6:15). For Paul, and for us, sound doctrine is a door to worship.

Because of children's developmental levels, we choose carefully the doctrines we present to them. Very abstract doctrines like the Trinity, Justification, Election, and others that demand complex formal-operational thinking powers are best developed in early adolescence. We can, however, include in our content for worship many of the great concepts of Scripture such as sin, forgiveness, and salvation, which can be understood on a concrete level.

In all the array of Christian doctrines, probably none inspires awe and wonder like learning the attributes of God. Baxter feels this is as true of adults as it is of children: "The quality of worship depends on man's conception of the character of God."[8] We can present to children of every age the wonderful God of the Bible. The Psalms and narrative portions of the Scripture are full of the glories of His person and the wonders of His dealings with men. Children, as natural worshipers, respond to stories of God as Creator, as Savior, and as the All-powerful, All-knowing, and All-compassionate Father. Thus, instead of dwelling upon interesting or exciting details of a Bible story, stress in your worship message how the character of God is shown in the story. Magnify His acts of love and His concern for His people. Present the Savior in His infinite tenderness and mighty power. When Jesus is lifted up, we are told in John 12:32, all hearts, including children's will be drawn to Him.

Other church doctrines which should receive attention in children's church include the Christian ordinances of communion and baptism. Older primaries and juniors should understand the origins of these symbolic acts, although some of the deeper meanings will not be fully appreciated until later.

3. *Evangelism.* Another word translated "to preach" in our Bibles is *euangelidzo,* meaning to tell the Good News, to evangelize. The children's church service is an appropriate place to present the gospel to children in a way they can understand. Preschool children should hear of God's unconditional love for them. School-age children are often ready to respond to the story of salvation when it is presented in the concrete terms of the gospel accounts: God sent His Son to earth because He loved us; Jesus lived among men to show us how to live; He died to take the punishment for the sins we do every day, and rose again to promise us life with Him forever. He wants to forgive us and make us members of His family.

These are not concepts that should be repeated every Sunday. The gospel too often becomes a trite set of statements to which children give unthinking assent. The way of salvation loses its impact if it is no more than pat answers to the teacher's questions. Instead, an evangelistic message should grow organically from the Scripture passage. It should be presented with all the care, drama, and feeling a great message deserves and in a way that will inspire, though not coerce, a response. Special prayer and meticulous preparation should precede any message with an evangelistic aim. It is frightening to think of the possible harm done by shoddy and thoughtless invitations which are easy for listeners to ignore or reject. Such "evangelism" may innoculate children against catching the real thing—an encounter with Jesus that changes them forever.

4. *Christian Living.* ". . .If there is any fellowship of the Spirit," pleads the apostle, "if any affection and compassion, make my joy complete by being of the same mind, maintaining the same love, united in spirit, intent on one purpose. Do nothing from selfishness or empty conceit, but with humility of mind let each of you regard one another as more important than himself" (Phil. 2:1-3, NASB).

Is it possible to forge a Christian society in a pagan milieu? The churches of Paul's day existed in an environment hostile to Christian morals and values—a world very much like our own. Yet Paul could envision a close-knit fellowship of people who knew God and cared for one another. Children's church should aim for such a fellowship. It should be a laboratory for Christian living and an environment for Christian worship. Here children can learn to be "kind one to another, tenderhearted, forgiving. . ." as they see this life style modeled in others.

Children need to understand how God intends us to relate to one another. They need to experience "holy living" as healthy living—to know that behavior consistent with God's commands produces joyful people, able to cope with life's problems as well as enjoy its pleasures. Our worship messages should enlighten the practical, day-to-day experiences of a child's life. God's Word can speak to a boy's struggle with tough kids on the playground; it can enhance his delight in family outings and holiday celebrations; it can instruct him in getting along with his friends and help him love his sister or brother. Above all, it can imbue him with a sense of self-worth: he is infinitely important to God.

When grief or tragedy occur, our Bible messages must help children know they do not confront darkness alone. The Good Shepherd is One who walks with us, even through the valley of the shadow of death. When life shines with happy experiences, we can help children be thankful to the One who gives us richly all things to enjoy. All these can emerge in the content of our worship messages.

5. *Missions.* Christian responsibility extends to the church worldwide and to the peoples of other lands and cultures who have not known Christ. Missions should be a regular component of the church-time curriculum. Christian and Missionary Alliance churches have a valuable resource for presenting missions. *The Alliance World,* a quarterly package of missions programs for children, youth, and adults includes pictures, projects, and maps of Alliance fields. A section designed for children's

church provides a fully developed missions emphasis for each month of the year. Missionary speakers should be included in the worship program whenever possible. This is a time when children's hearts can be reached with messages that challenge commitment.

6. *The Church Year.* The church-time program offers an ideal opportunity to celebrate events of the Christian calendar. The Advent and Easter seasons can be highlighted over several weeks of the winter and spring. Harvest, Thanksgiving, and Pentecost are other feasts which many churches observe. A greal deal of supplementary curricular material is available for seasonal use. See the publishers listed in the Appendix.

Methods for the Worship Message

What is the best way to present the message in a children's worship service? Which method most effectively draws the listener into the subject, stimulates the mind, captures the affections, and challenges the will? Storytelling, the oldest teaching method known to man, best meets these requirements. It is the method Jesus used more powerfully than any other. For centuries after Christ, until Gutenberg invented his press, it was the major means of educating the masses in biblical knowledge. Today the story, in all its forms and varieties, remains the surest way to captivate and move your young learners.

Storytelling

The storyteller who follows Jesus' example and uses concrete words, vivid images, and human emotion cannot fail to enthrall his listeners. The stories Jesus told pulsate with human drama. The same woes, trials, and joys fill today's newspaper: runaway sons, businessmen mugged on the road, marriages, deaths, possessions lost and found, celebrations, and personal disasters. Never vague and seldom abstract, Jesus used word-pictures and strong action verbs in His stories. The vine growers did not "perform a reprehensible crime"; they killed the owner's son and threw him out of the vineyard! The shepherd put the foundling "on his shoulders, rejoicing." The prodigal hungered to fill his belly with the pigs' husks, and the Samaritan dressed the victim's wounds with oil and wine. These are events we can see, feel, smell, and taste; these are people we can visualize.

With the right story the teller touches the emotions, arousing fear, love, anger, admiration, enthusiasm. A good story teaches without seeming to; the listener feels with the character and experiences everything he does. The truth is implicit in the action: no moral need be tacked on, nor lesson applied when the story unfolds properly. The way the teller uses his eyes, face, voice, and body conveys the message better than any visual aid. Every leader of children should master the storytelling art, and use it often in the worship service.

Drama

Drama is a storytelling technique in which the action is portrayed rather than described. For young children especially, dramatization is hard to beat as a means of communication.

The lesson one morning was on Jesus and Nicodemus. It introduced the concept of the new birth—not an easy one to present to five-year-olds. Just before the story was to begin, the teacher donned a long shawl, draping it over her head. She took a candlestick from the closet and lit a flame.

Deliberately, she walked toward the front of the group, mounted imaginary stairs and knocked on an invisible entrance. She greeted Jesus and introduced herself as Nicodemus. As the teacher carried on a one-way conversation with Jesus, the story of that long-ago night was relived by every child. They shared Nicodemus's confusion about what it meant to be born again, and smiled with him at the happy discovery that Jesus came not to punish him, but to offer him everlasting life.[9]

Teacher-led drama is an excellent method of presenting the worship message. Two or three adults may be needed, and sometimes a child can play a part. Older children can dramatize a Bible story themselves very effectively. In *Children Can Worship*, the author tells how a group of juniors in simple costumes portrayed the Easter story. The children's skit showed how the disciples might have recalled the Resurrection one year later.

> As they went toward the garden the women told of their surprise and shock at finding the angel there, and how they ran to tell the disciples. Peter and John recounted how they went to the tomb. And then several recalled how the Lord had come right through the closed door that evening and what He had said and done. The group concluded with a joint enthusiastic statement, Christ is risen indeed![10]

Puppet plays, skits, and shadow screens are other ways of dramatizing the message, as explained in Chapter 6. Teachers should use these techniques often enough to provide a good pattern for children. Teacher productions can be more polished and controlled and may be more reliable in attaining a desired objective. However, there is much to be gained in having children plan and produce dramatizations at regular intervals.

Visual Methods

To fulfill the purpose of proclamation, the worship leader depends most often on teacher-centered methods of presentation which can best evoke a response of worship or commitment. (For teacher-centered methods, see chart on page 175.) Both projected and non-projected visuals are excellent aids in such a presentation. Large pictures or flashcard stories focus attention and can illumine obscure concepts. Illustrated books on the Bible help children visualize Bible events. Good paintings, prints, and photographs can be profoundly moving. Keep a file of these in easy access and use them often.

Films, filmstrips, and slides provide alternate means of telling a story or of focusing on a concept. The large, colorful image creates a strong impact; sound tracks add another dimension to film and should be used whenever possible. The overhead projector should not be ignored as a visual means of telling a story. Preparing pictures on transparencies makes it possible to use the overhead as a stage on which the story action is played out. Transparencies provide color, a large image, and great flexibility. See the Christian Education Monograph, "Making Your Own Transparencies" listed in the Appendix for help in using this technique.

Flannelgraph has proved itself over half a century as an effective teaching method, as popular with children as it is with teachers. It is a simple and inexpensive way to vary the message format since most of the major stories of the Bible have been produced in flannelgraph. Innovations with double-board figures and cassette tape sound tracks are attractive features which can keep this "old standby" new and fresh.

Choose carefully the method and materials you will use for each Sunday's message. Not every good teaching method lends itself to worship. Discussion, learning centers, research projects—these are excellent methods for learning but less likely to move persons emotionally or inspire them to awe and wonder. In the brief time you or your helpers have to bring the worship message, strive to draw from the hearers a response to God. Those who bring the message stand in the role of the preacher—the herald proclaiming Good News. In this role as in all others, those of us who lead children must work and pray for vision, imagination, and wisdom.

The opening chapters of this book argued for the acceptability of children and their worship: Jesus accepts children as they are, welcomes their praise, and calls us to nurture them in the faith. Succeeding chapters discussed how to instruct them in worship "according to their way," according to the level of maturity they have attained.

Our children come to us each Sunday different than they were the week before. In the intervening days as a result of their own biology and their contact with society they have changed and grown. Have they matured spiritually as well? If their environment has provided the proper stimulus, yes. For these children, the spiritual environment of the home is supported and enhanced by the church program. For many others, probably more than we think, the hours between 9:30 and 12:00 on Sunday provide the only Christian environment they know. Do our activities, methods, resources, and affection meet their overwhelming needs? Do our prayers sustain them?

We have a message that can change the world. It will transform the lives of children and families who receive it. Believing this, let us expend every effort, unearth every talent, master every method that will let us fulfill our task of helping children worship God in all their words and ways.

Notes

1. Margeret Self, ed., *Sing to the Lord* (Glendale: Praise Books [GL], 1976), #3, #33.
2. *Hymns of the Christian Life* (Harrisburg: Christian Publications, Inc., 1978).
3. Paul H. Vieth, *Worship in Christian Education* (Philadelphia: United Church Press, 1965), p. 39.
4. Mary LeBar, *Children Can Worship* (Wheaton: Victor Books/Scripture Press, 1976), p. 87.
5. Kamir Olson, a specialist in teaching young children, led this session at Simpson Memorial Church, Nyack, NY.
6. LeBar, *Children Can Worship*, p. 21.
7. For more on this subject, see "Teaching: the Necessary Gift," *The Alliance Teacher* (Summer 1980), p. 3.
8. Baxter, *Learning to Worship*, p. 83.
9. Marjorie Cowles (Mrs. H. Robert,) taught this lesson in the kindergarten of Simpson Memorial Church.
10. LeBar, *Children Can Worship*, p. 97.

Appendix

Resources for Children's Church

An inexhaustible array of possible resources exists on which church teachers can draw. Local Christian bookstores, public libraries, and publishers' catalogs provide new products each year. Included here are items selected on the basis of (1) their suitability to the children's worship program, and (2) the author's familiarity with the product. Other good materials are available which I have not had opportunity to use or review. Investigate these and the many new products which continually arrive on the market.*

Curriculum and Content for Worship Programs

In addition to the three curriculums reviewed in Chapter 4, pages 78-80, these provide complete worship programs:

Children's Worship Service Helps. Convention Press. 127 Ninth Avenue North, Nashville, TN 37234.

Huttar, Leora. *Church Time for Preschoolers.* Denver: Accent Books.

Supplementary content for children's church may be drawn from the following sources. (Still other sources are listed under Visual Aids.) Each contains a series of lessons which might provide basic content for several worship programs. Check with Sunday school curriculum to be sure content does not overlap or repeat.

Biblegrams. Child Evangelism Fellowship. Warrenton: CEF Series of flannelgraph lessons on each Bible story.

Canon Bible Filmstrips. 406 Gunderson, Box 1616, Wheaton, IL 60187. Filmstrips and records of Old and New Testament stories. Discussion guides.

Coleman, William. The Good Night Book. Minneapolis: Bethany Fellowship, Inc. Devotional messages.

Gospel Graphs: Choosing, Giving, Helping, Loving, Obeying, Whosoever's House. Wheaton: Victor Books/Scripture Press. Younger children.

Keithahn, Mary Nelson. All about Paul. Scottsdale, AZ, National Teacher Education Project, (7214 E. Granada Road. 85257). Learning centers and activities for several months. Older children.

Equipment and Supplies

Doan, Eleanor. Make It Yourself Equipment Encyclopedia. Glendale: Gospel Light/Regal Books.

How to Build Equipment for Children's Departments. Diagrams and Instructions. Materials Services Department, 127 Ninth Avenue North, Nashville, TN 37234.

Posters, Maps, Decorations—send for catalogs:

    Argus Communications, 7440 Natchez Ave., Niles, IL 60648.

    National Geographic Society, 1146 16th St. NW, Washington, DC 20036.

    Wright Studio, 5264 Brookeville Road, Indianapolis, IN 46219.

Supply Catalogs:

    Christian Publications, Inc., 25 S. 10th Street, P.O. Box 3404, Harrisburg, PA 17105.

    Special equipment for children's rooms. Constructive Playthings, 2008 W. 103 Terr. Leawood, KS 66206.

Evangelism

Heerman, Keith. *Outreach to Children.* ICL concept book, Glendale, CA 91200.

Discovery Books, *Who Cares? He Cares!, Why Should I?* and other booklets for children. Wheaton: Victor Books/Scripture Press.

Good News booklet. (Four Spiritual Laws for Children) Campus Crusade for Christ, San Bernardino, CA 92414. Junior age.

How to Become God's Child and Live in His Family. Wheaton: Victor Books/Scripture Press.

LeBar, Mary. *The Best Family of All.* Wheaton: Victor Books/Scripture Press.

Games and Puzzles

All Occasion Finger Plays for Young Children: Bible Finger Plays for Young Children. Cincinnati: Standard Publishing.

Beegle, Shirley. *Bible Game Ideas.* Cincinnati: Standard Publishing.

Bible Puzzlers Grades 3-6 and *Bible Puzzlers Grades 1-3.* Also *Pictures and Puzzles Grades 4-6.* Cincinnati: Standard Publishing. Pressure-Fax duplicating masters.

Bible Picture Pairs and *Bible ABC Pairs,* ages 3-7. Cincinnati: Standard Publishing.

Fuzzy Felt Bible Stories and *Fuzzy Felt Pets.* Cincinnati: Standard Publishing.

Schaupp, Jack. *Creating and Playing Games with Students.* Nashville: Abingdon Press.

Scripture Activity Books—*Noah, Joseph, Moses, Ruth, David.* Inexpensive books for children, grades 3-6. American Bible Society, 1865 Broadway, New York, NY 10023.

Handcraft and Art Projects

Beegle, Shirley. *Craft Ideas for All Ages.* Cincinnati: Standard Publishing.

Knoderer, Paula. *Created in Faith.* Seventy-five handcraft projects of Christian symbols. St. Louis: Concordia Publishing House.

Reese, Loretta A. *54 Crafts with Easy Patterns.* Cincinnati: Standard Publishing.

Rowen, Dolores. *Easy to Make Crafts.* For children ages 3 to 11. Glendale: Gospel Light/Regal Books.

Self, Margeret. *Now What Can We Do?* Glendale: Gospel Light/Regal Books.

Yoder, Glee. *Take It from Here.* Valley Forge: Judson Press.

Music

Smith, Barbara and Charles. *The Non-Musicians Guide to Children's Music.* ICL concept book. Glendale: Gospel Light/Regal Books.

Songbooks:
> *Little Ones Sing* (revised) and *Sing to the Lord.* Glendale: Praise Book, Gospel Light/Regal Books.
>
> *Motions 'N Music.* For Bible Stories. Thirty-three musical activities for young children, with tapes. Wheaton: Victor Books/Scripture Press.
>
> *Primaries and Juniors Sing.* Elgin: David C. Cook Publishing Company.
>
> *Young Children Sing* and *Primaries Sing.* Wheaton: Victor Books/Scripture Press.

Recordings:
> Gaither, Bill and Gloria. *Especially for Children* Series. Nashville: Impact Books/Div. J. T. Benson.
>
> *God's Four Seasons.* Activity music. Wheaton: Victor Books/Scripture Press.

>*I Worship When I Sing.* Songs for children 6 to 8. Nashville: Broadman Press.
>
>*Music for Quiet Times.* Nashville: Broadman Press.
>
>*Praising God Together.* Songs for children 4 to 5. Nashville: Broadman Press.

Teaching Worship through Music:
>*Music in Bible Times Picture Set.* 9" x 12" color pictures. Wheaton: Victor Books/Scripture Press.

Musical Instruments:
>*Constructive Playthings* Catalog. 2008 W. 103 Terrace. Leawood, KS 66206.

Special Children

>Clark, D. Dahl, J. and Gonsenboch, L. *Teach Me, Please Teach Me.* Elgin: David C. Cook Publishing Company.
>
>Hawley, Gloria. *How to Teach the Mentally Retarded.* Wheaton: Victor Books/Scripture Press.
>
>*Happytime Course.* Fifty-two lessons for teaching the retarded. *Leader's Guide.* Bible stories, visuals, and music. Wheaton: Victor Books/Scripture Press.
>
>*Multi-Media Training Package.* Three filmstrips and audio cassettes. Borrow from Jim Pierson, Consultant, Special Education, 325 Crossfield Drive, Knoxville, TN 37920.
>
>*Special Education Activity Packet.* Includes Sing-Look-Do Songbook, Bible People Pairs Puzzle, Creative Crafts, and other supplies. Cincinnati: Standard Publishing.

Teacher Development

Leading Children's Church:
>Baxter, Edna M. *Learning to Worship.* Valley Forge:

Judson Press.

Larson, Jim. *Church Time for Children.* Glendale: Gospel Light/Regal Books.

LeBar, Mary. *Children Can Worship.* Wheaton: Victor Books/Scripture Press.

Teaching Methodology:

Crabtree, June. *Learning Center Ideas* and *Teach 'Em Like God Made 'Em.* Cincinnati: Standard Publishing.

Gangel, Kenneth. *Twenty-four Ways to Improve Your Teaching.* Wheaton: Victor Books/Scripture Press.

Griggs, Pat and Donald. *Creative Activities in Church Education* and *Twenty Ways to Use Drama in Teaching the Bible.* Nashville: Abingdon Press.

Liu, Sarah, and Vittitow, Mary. *Creative Bible Activities for Children.* Wheaton: Victor Books/Scripture Press.

Wilt, Joy. *Taste and Smell: 40 Tasting and Smelling Experiences for Children,* and other books on the senses. Waco: Word Books Publishers.

Visual Aids

Barret, Ethel. *Stories to Grow On* Series. Books and cassettes—*Blister Lamb, Buzz Bee,* etc. Teaching Christian values to young children. Glendale: Gospel Light/Regal Books.

Bible Story Filmstrips, Moody Institute of Science, 1200 E. Washington Blvd., Whittier, CA 90606. Old Testament stories—write for catalog.

Christian Teaching Resources. Transparency and duplicating books and Wipe-Clean cards on Bible History, Bible Background, Gifts from God, Friends of God, Life of Jesus, etc. St. Louis: Milliken Publishing Company.

Life of Jesus Teaching Pictures. Five sets by Francis and Richard Hook. Elgin: David C. Cook Publishing Company.

Teacher-made visuals:

Darkes, Anna Sue. *How to Make and Use Overhead Transparencies.* Chicago: Moody Press.

Doan, Eleanor. *Pattern Encyclopedia* and *Visual Aid Encyclopedia.* Glendale: Gospel Light/Regal Books.

Green, Lee. *Teaching Tools You Can Make.* Wheaton: Victor Books/Scripture Press.

McGuirk, Don. *Better Media for Less Money,* vols. 1 & 2. Scottsdale, National Teacher Education Project, 7214 Granada Road, Scottsdale, AZ 85257.

Olson, Kamir. "Make Your Own Overhead Transparencies." Christian Education Monograph. Harrisburg: Christian Publications, Inc.

Rodin, Shelley. *When Puppets Talk Everybody Listens.* Wheaton: Victor Books/Scripture Press.

Rottman, Fran. *Easy to Make Puppets and How to Use Them.* (Early Childhood), (Children/Youth). Glendale: Gospel Light/Regal Books.

Wilt, Joy and Hurn, G. & J. *Puppets with Pizazz* and *More Puppets with Pizazz.* Waco: Word Books Publishers.

Audio-visual materials for creative projects: write-on slides, doodle film, etc. Educational Technical Services Company, P.O. Box 407, Chatham, NJ 07928.

*Except where an address is included, all items on this Resources list may be ordered from Christian Publications, Inc., 25 S. 10th Street, P.O. Box 3404, Harrisburg, PA 17105.

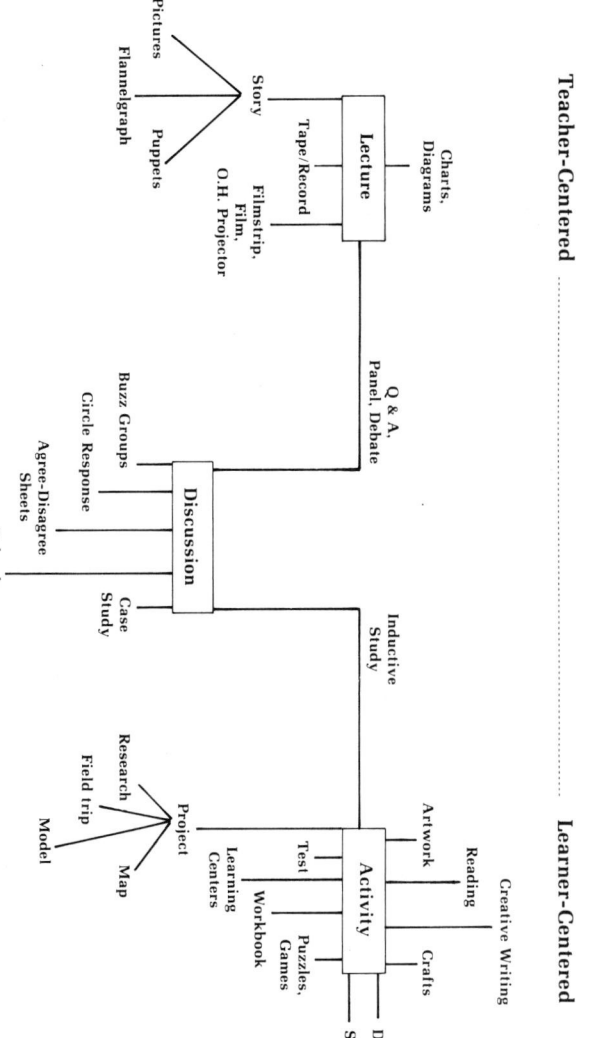

BV
1522
.W53
1981